Enabling the Elderly

SUNY Series on Aging

Sheldon S. Tobin and *Edmund Sherman,* EDITORS

ENABLING THE ELDERLY

*Religious Institutions
within the
Community Service System*

Sheldon S. Tobin
James W. Ellor
and
Susan M. Anderson-Ray

State University of New York Press

Published by
State University of New York Press, Albany

©1986 State University of New York

Printed in the United States of America

For information, address State University of New York
Press, State University Plaza, Albany, N.Y. 12246

Library of Congress Cataloging in Publication Data

Tobin, Sheldon S.
   Enabling the elderly.

   (SUNY series on aging)
   Bibliography: p. 177
   1. Church work with the aged. I. Ellor, James W.
II. Anderson-Ray, Susan M. III. Title.
BV4435.T63 1986   259′.3   86-5693
ISBN 0-88706-334-9
ISBN 0-88706-335-7 (pbk.)

10 9 8 7 6 5 4 3 2

Contents

Preface   vii

Part I. The Context   1

Chapter 1.   Aging in Modern Society   3
Chapter 2.   Spiritual Well-Being and Holistic
              Programs with the Elderly   15
Chapter 3.   Church and Synagogue in
              Programming with the Aging   27
Chapter 4.   Community Church: An Example of
              Decision Making in Action   39

Part II. Serving Older People in a Variety of Settings   61

Chapter 5.   The Well-Elderly in the Community   63
Chapter 6.   Enabling the Homebound   75
Chapter 7.   Outreach to Nursing Home Residents   97
Chapter 8.   Living with the Dying   121

**Part III. Religious Institutions and the
Service System**   141

Chapter 9.   Working Together   143
Chapter 10.   A Model for Increasing Interaction
              among Churches, Synagogues,
              and Social Agencies   159

Epilogue   175

References   177

Index of Proper Names   187

Subject Index   189

Preface

Religious institutions are important to the well-being of the elderly. Beyond providing spiritual direction and solace, church and synagogue can, and do, provide other functions that enable the elderly to remain active contributors to their community and to retain a sense of continuity in their lives. The enabling functions of church and synagogue are particularly important for the elderly because of losses associated with advancing age and because the elderly are more religious than younger generations. Indeed, it is not unusual for a large percentage of congregations to be older people. Beyond Biblical imperatives to provide special concern for the elderly is the reality of the unique contribution church and synagogue can make to the well-being of the elderly.

Yet religious institutions cannot address all the needs of the elderly. Never before has there been an aging society, and now one of every nine Americans is sixty-five years of age or over. Obviously, among this large and heterogeneous group are individuals with a diversity of unmet needs. Still, it must be recognized that spiritual well-being moves beyond a religious focus to encompass concern for the wholeness of the individual and to a concern for the quality of life of each individual. Thus, it is essential that church and synagogue work both independently and in collaboration with other social institutions to seek to provide for the full range of human needs. Religious institutions must work with secular institutions, on the one hand, to meet needs that appear to be less than religious in nature and, on the other hand, to infuse a sense of the spiritual into the service provision to the elderly by secular institutions.

Innovation is necessary. When we began our exploration ten years ago on how to enhance collaboration among religious institutions and secular service providers, little was known and even less was being done. Now, fortunately, a variety of activities exists in communities throughout the country. The Interfaith Volunteer Caregivers Program, for example, was developed by the Robert Wood Johnson Foundation and co-sponsored by the National Interfaith Coalition on Aging, to fund twenty-five community initiatives to enable impaired elderly to remain at home. The intent of those initiatives is not to substitute for local health professionals but, rather, to supplement their provision of care.

Our work began with an investigation by Lucy Steinitz for her doctoral dissertation of the ways in which churches and synagogues do and do not collaborate with service agencies on behalf of the elderly. When her study indicated a serious lack of collaboration, we developed an action project, "Enhancing the Church and Synagogue as Service Provider to the Elderly," that was funded by the Retirement Research Foundation for three years. Essentially, therefore, this book represents our experience over a ten-year period of exploring how church and synagogue, as well as clergy, provide spiritual well-being to the elderly and, also, the potential for church and synagogue to collaborate with a diversity of service agencies in a variety of communities and settings to enable the elderly to maximize their quality of life.

We shall, in Part I, first provide a foundation for understanding the role of religious institutions within the community service system. We begin by discussing aging in modern society; continue by clarifying the meaning of spiritual well-being and holistic programs for the elderly; then turn to specifics regarding church and synagogue in proper programming with the aging; and, finally, provide an example of program development in one church (actually, a composite of several with which we have worked).

Then, in Part II, we consider the elderly in a variety of settings: the well-elderly in the community, the homebound elderly, elderly who reside in nursing homes, and the dying. In each of these four chapters, we first discuss the status and needs of the target group, then the kinds of approaches we must consider if we are to enable the elderly to function better and to be themselves, and, finally, specific proposals for enhancing the holistic quality of their lives. Results of studies that we have undertaken as part of our project are incorporated into each of the four chapters.

Finally, in Part III, we focus explicitly on church and synagogue within the service system. In the first of two chapters, we discuss the benefits and the obstacles to collaboration with other religious institutions and with human service agencies. Included are approaches to working together. In the second chapter of this section, and the final chapter in the book, we discuss the model that we developed to facilitate enhancement of cooperation among churches, synagogue, and service agencies, and we report on the success of our efforts to enhance collaboration in different kinds of communities.

The organization of this manuscript emerged from two kinds of goals. First, we wished to synthesize the knowledge we have gained with the knowledge of others regarding the complexity and interaction of spiritual and other needs among elderly in a variety of life circumstances and settings. Second, we wished to translate this knowledge into general and specific approaches to assisting members of religious institutions and service agencies in creating meaningful opportunities for enabling the elderly to optimize their quality of life. A particular concern of ours, as noted earlier, has been the lack of collaborative efforts between religious and secular institutions in this enabling process; thus, we have explicitly focused on ways of enhancing collaboration. The rationale for this focus will become apparent, if it is not already from readers' past experiences. In blending and balancing the rationals with concrete suggestions for actions, we have attempted to write a book that is easily understood by lay persons, as well as by professionals unconversant with either gerontology or spiritual well-being. The knowledgeable reader should not misinterpret our simplification of language, nor our concrete suggestions for action, as a simplistic approach to complex theoretical and applied issues. Indeed, our major challenge was to simplify without being simplistic.

Our team benefitted from its diversity: the first author is a Jewish gerontologist who has trained as a social scientist, the second author is an MSW social worker and a Presbyterian minister with a Doctorate in Divinity, and the third author is Lutheran and also an MSW social worker. Adding to our diversity were our diligent project assistants who came from varied religious and cultural backgrounds. We are most thankful to Julie Baltz, Kay Cammaron, Jeff Finkbiner, Jean Gray-Ehnert, Robin Goldberg, Greg Jones, Marci Jensen, Michael Kuchinsky, Grace Lee, Mary Nelson, Sally O'Leary and Kathy Reed for their talent and commitment. Because the staff members of so many churches, synagogues, and social service agencies contributed to our work, we cannot thank them all. We are, however, particularly grateful to Reverend Michael Barker, Tobi Ehrenpreis, Val Ensalaco, Sherry Kraft and Reverend Bryan Sickbert. Additionally, the seminal work of Lucy Steinitz on the role of clergy in services to the elderly in one community formed the basis for our project. A special acknowledgement is due Professor Perry LeFevre of the Chicago Theological Seminary and Phyllis Harmann, "rebbitzan," who took precious time away from their everyday responsibilities to read an early draft and provide invaluable criticism. In turn, for finalization of the manuscript we appreciate and are thankful to Lee Morgan-Davie for her editorial assistance and to Barbara Rogers, Gail Texter, and Barbara J. Kelly for their fine secretarial expertise.

A special debt is owed Reverend Donald F. Clingan, D. Min., who encouraged us to write this book and whose book *Aging Persons in the Community of Faith* was, in part, a model for ours. Beyond his encouragement was the inspiration he provided to us because of his dedication to enhancing the well-being of the elderly.

To the Retirement Research Foundation which funded our project, we hope that this volume confirms the Foundation's assessment of the meaningfulness of our work for the elderly. We are especially grateful to Marilyn Hennessy, Executive Director of the Foundation, for her encouragement and her sensitivity to the complex set of issues we have confronted in attempting to enhance the church and synagogue as service providers for the elderly.

Part I

The Context

Who are the aging? What does it mean to age in modern society? Are elderly alienated from their familes? From their community? From their church and synagogue? How has society responded to the needs of the aging? These are the kinds of questions addressed in Chapter 1, "Aging in Modern Society," the first of four chapters defining the context of church and synagogue in enabling the elderly.

In Chapter 2, entitled "Spiritual Well-Being and Holistic Programs with the Elderly," we discuss and develop a holistic approach to working with the elderly.

Next in Chapter 3, we turn to "Church and Synagogue in Programming With the Elderly," examining the justification for involvement inservice for older people and potential roles for the church and synagogue in working with older people.

Finally, in Chapter 4, we discuss "Community Church" as an example of a church seeking to expand its efforts to serve and enable older people.

Hopefully, this section will set the tone for the rest of the book. The issues we address in the first four chapters will begin to develop the principles and guidelines for creating a caring community for the elderly in congregations and with service providers and, also, assist in the understanding of the role of social advocacy in ministry to, and with, the elderly.

1

Chapter One

Aging in Modern Society

Growing older is a process that begins at birth and ends with death. When a child reaches the age of ten, he or she has grown older, just as a man of eighty has grown and accommodated a long life of experience. People do not cross a boundary and suddenly become "old." There is not an age at which people cease being individuals with the full range of human characteristics and become instead one homogeneous group labelled "old people." Instead, as people age, they retain their uniqueness and individuality.

Given the differences among people, gerontologists (those who study processes of growing older) have asked whether there is anything shared by all people as they grow older. Certainly, there are common biological changes that accompany the aging process, such as graying, wrinkling, some loss of hearing and vision, and loss of strength. Psychological changes are less obvious, but these, too, are present in most people as they grow older. Sometime during their forties or fifties, most people become aware that life is finite. From this point on, they do not simply count how many years they have lived but also how many years they have left. A process of taking stock begins, in which each person asks whether he or she has achieved what has been hoped to be achieved in life. This kind of shift in thoughts about self has been labelled by Neugarten (1977) as a shift toward interiority. Some respond to the shift with a sense of

begins

40-50

3

satisfaction, whereas others become upset and feel that life has passed them by. Among those with the latter kind of crisis are individuals who seek a "lost youth." Some suddenly become depressed, others leave spouse and family. The majority, however, accepts life without a midlife crisis.

A different kind of psychological crisis can be seen in the later years. As people approach their seventies and eighties, death becomes a closer reality. Current evidence suggests that in these older years, one's own death becomes accepted (Munnichs, 1966). Yet, while one's personal death may be accepted, there are certainly fears related to dying alone or dying with pain.

The most critical task among the very old is to retain a sense of identity when confronting physical decline and the loss of loved ones. Stated another way, the task of the very old is to maintain a sense of sameness when confronted with all the losses associated with advancing age (Lieberman and Tobin, 1983). Because the human spirit is so remarkable, the typical person is able to maintain a sense of self. For most, the past becomes a source of assurance that one is still the same person. Current interactions also become a way to reaffirm a continuity of self in spite of changes. Further, personal faith, as well as participation in a church or synagogue, becomes important in supporting the understanding that one is the same person and will remain so throughout time. Not to be minimized in the affirmation of personal identity is the role of religious symbols, such as prayer books, religious paintings, Christmas nativities, and menorahs. Additionally, religious rituals, such as baptisms, circumcisions, bar mitzvahs, confirmations, weddings, and funerals, are an important part of life that have special meaning in assuring continuity between the past and present.

The Young-Old and the Old-Old

Gerontologists have suggested that, with the growing numbers of older people, it is useful to think of two

categories of elderly: the "young-old" and the "old-old."
Neugarten (1974) has defined the young-old as those people over the age of fifty-five who are relatively healthy, affluent, and free from traditional family and work responsibilities. Increasingly, this has become a well-educated
group of individuals who remain socially and politically active. The old-old, in contrast, are generally identified as people of advanced old age who suffer declining health, decrea-
ing financial resources, and more limited social involvement.
Those over the age of seventy-five often can be characterized
in this manner. It is important to stress that age alone does
not distinguish the young-old from the old-old. The more
useful distinction lies in the change in health and social involvement. Further, the types of support needed by each of
these two groups are quite different.

Whereas now slightly less than 12 percent of the population is sixty-five and over, by 2020 the elderly may comprise
close to 20 percent, depending on birthrates during the inter-
vening years (see, for example, Neugarten, 1982). Moreover,
it is the oldest among the elderly that are increasing at the
fastest rate. Now, about 40 percent of the elderly are over
seventy-five, with 5 percent over eighty-five. The projections
for the year 2020 suggest that nearly 60 percent of those sixty-
five and over will be over seventy-five and as many as 15 percent will be over eighty-five years of age. Until advanced old
age, the elderly maintain relatively good health and remain
active contributors to their families and communities. Then,
in the final years of life, they are likely to suffer from a variety
of infirmities and losses.

Since most of the young-old are likely to be relatively
healthy, fairly well educated and reasonably financially
secure, their needs and interests tend to be broad and varied.
Generally, these include participation in activities which provide for meaningful use of leisure time, opportunities for
religious, social and civic involvement, including leadership,
and access to health care which maintains their good physical
and mental status. Housing needs may change for those who
desire living close to those of a similar age. Assistance with
general transportation needs may also be a concern for some

of these seniors, since most are willing and able to participate in a full range of civic, religious, and social activities.

A maximum number of options to meet the diversity of these needs is desirable. For example, the newly retired individual should be able to choose from a range of possibilities the way in which he or she wishes to spend time. Opportunities for religious and community participation and public service, as well as for personal fulfillment, should be expanded. Such involvement could lessen significantly the common "retirement crisis." As it is today, many retired persons must structure their time largely on an ad hoc basis, often leaving them with the feeling of being forgotten by society and useless.

The old-old have a strikingly different set of needs. As mentioned earlier, these individuals are generally less healthy and vigorous then the young-old. They continue to need a variety of options for productive ways to use their leisure time, as well as meaningful religious, community, and public service roles. However, their ability to engage in these activities depends on their health status and enabling services. The majority of the old-old live independently but need both health and social services, as well as special adaptations in their physical environment to enable them to function as fully as possible.

Aging in the Family

Biological and psychological changes do not occur separate from one's social environment. The family is one of the most important components in the social environment throughout life. Contrary to some stereotypes, the elderly are not abandoned by their families. However, the structure of the family has changed dramatically in the twentieth century! For example, at the turn of the last century, there was no empty nest. That is, children were likely to be at home when a woman became a widow in her forties or fifties. Those left at home were obliged to care for mother. Often the youngest daughter sacrificed marriage in order to care for her parent. Now, the scenario is different. Women who want to have families tend to have their children by their mid-twenties. By the time these women reach forties, their children leave home to being new careers and/or families. Thereafter, wives and husbands can anticipate thirty or forty years of life together without children under the same roof. Together, spouses watch the birth of grandchildren and great-grandchildren, and obtain great joy in observing and participating with the second, third, and even fourth generations.

Although there is a physical separateness of generations, the commitment to care for family members has not decreased. Four of five older people still live within one-half hour drive from at least one child (see Sussman, 1985, and Troll, Miller and Atchley, 1979, for reviews of family life of the elderly). Today, when the frailty and illness of aging parents becomes a problem, their children still become concerned with the needs of their parents. As one woman in her middle years said: "Just when I finished child-caring, I have to worry about caring for my parents." In one sense, parent-caring has become a general issue in our society because people are living longer. With the conquering of many infectious diseases and other advances in health and medical care, people are surviving to more advanced ages. A woman who reaches sixty-five can expect to live more than twenty years longer, a man to live only one or two years less! Indeed, because of the lengthening of life, a new phenomenon has occurred in which retired persons have aging parents to whom they are providing care. Yet, to survive until advanced old age often means to survive with many chronic impairments which increase dependence on others. For example, conquering the three leading causes of death (cancer, stroke, and heart disease) would probably add eleven or twelve more years to the average life, but, at the same time, it would probably increase skeletal infirmities and mental impairments among the very old.

The current focus on parent-caring in the popular literature unfortunately too often ignores the role of wives in caring for disabled husbands. Most American women marry men older than themselves. Further, these women generally live longer than men. Because of these two factors, it is likely that many elderly women will be caring for a sick and dying husband. After being widowed, it is not uncommon for a women to move into the home of a child. Typically, she is still cared for by a daughter. We should not forget, however, that, if the mother is in her eighties or nineties, the daughter may be in her sixties or seventies and also struggling with the changes associated with her own aging. In addition, many of these daughters are caring for two infirmed elderly parents.

Aging in Communities

As people age, they tend to remain in their communities. It is falsely assumed by most that elderly persons move to retirement communities in warmer climates. Some do, but most do not. Most elderly "age-in-place," remaining in the community in which they reared their children (see, for example, Golant, 1984). In this mobile society, however, children are likely to move away, first to college and then where employment opportunities take them. Because the young do move away, in some communities the elderly may comprise over 20 percent of the population. The percentage of elderly throughout the country is closer to 11 percent.

The phenomenon of "aging-in-place" has important implications for church and synagogue, as well as for social service agencies. For example, suburban communities which were developed after World War II by young veterans rearing their families are now becoming communities of elderly. In turn, the churches and synagogues in these communities are likely to have congregations composed largely of persons in their sixties and seventies (Robb, 1981). Similarly, in inner-city neighborhoods, the elderly may have remained in the community when their children left. As the congregation ages, it will eventually reflect the changes of the local community. Although new members are of the same denomination, often they are of a different race, ethnic background, or socioeconomic class. This kind of change places a difficult burden on both the church or synagogue and the elderly.

As churches and synagogues become transformed by changes in the composition of communities, the elderly often feel disassociated from their former religious institutions. This, for example, is not uncommon when churches and synagogues merge or relocate. Many have feelings of being abandoned by the church or synagogue to which they contributed much and from which they derived a deep sense of spiritual wholeness. Moreover, a sense of distance can be intensified when new clergy come to replace the old. Elderly congregants often have shared a special relationship with an old minister, which developed over many years or even decades. In spite of these changes, many of the elderly continue to look toward their lifelong church or synagogue as a source of support and security.

Fortunately, while their house of worship and their community change, their lifelong neighbors and friends remain with them until separated by death. Together, old friends share memories, socialize, and sustain each other on a daily basis and in times of crisis. Neighbors and friends are indeed important for a sense of well-being and for mutual support and aid. These friendships are likely to have developed and to have deepened through shared church and synagogue activities. Particularly among the elderly, friends were probably selected because of common religious beliefs. It is also likely *church-sponsored living-facilities* that as a group of friends they expect their church or synagogue and related agencies to respond to them in times of need. When death is approaching, it is likely that they will turn to clergy for solace in easing the final journey.

Meeting the Needs of the Elderly

So far, we have covered some of the changes in individuals as they grow older, a distinction between the young-old and the old-old, aging in the family, and aging in the community. Now we shall begin to look systematically at the needs of older people and how these needs are met.

One way to understand the needs among the elderly is to consider three groups of elderly: those living relatively independently in the community, those living in the community who are severly impaired, and those living in nursing homes. As shown in Chart 1–1, the majority (estimated at 80 percent) of elderly live independently; about one in seven is severely impaired (estimated at 14 percent); and only a small percentage (about 6 percent) live in nursing homes. Some general characteristics of the three groups of elderly persons and their children, as well as how they change in aging are included in Chart 1–1.

Seven kinds of support services that each elderly person in each group may need can be identified, as shown in Chart 1–1: (1) health care, (2) mental health services, (3) in-home services, (4) social activites, (5) transportation, (6) housing, and (7) religious involvement and observances. The three groups of elderly differ in many of their needs. Let's look, for example, at health care. The elderly living independently in the community need preventive care and medical care that help maintain good health, whereas the impaired elderly need both acute medical care and home-health services. Lastly, elderly in nursing homes usually need twenty-four hour supervision and much nursing care. Regarding religious involvement and observance, the independent elderly can participate actively in church and synagogue, while the impaired who need health care, emotional support and spiritual assistance will need more specialized services brought into their homes. Those in nursing homes may be even more limited in their access to religious activities, yet they continue to need regular opportunities to observe their faith within the nursing home.

In considering the support services provided for the elderly, we need, at the very outset, to understand that there is not just one system providing services in this country. Some countries have a public service system that provides medical and social services to all the elderly who need these services. In contrast to many European countries, we have a relatively weak set of public services for the elderly. However, complementing public services are voluntary (not-for-profit) services and proprietary (for-profit) services. These three sets of services exist in every community.

Since the mid-1960s, numerous social service programs for the elderly have been developed by government and by voluntary and private agencies. In this context, social services refer to services that function for socialization, for counseling, and for coordinating or linking services on behalf of clients. Many programs to fulfill these functions have been supported by federal legislation under the Older Americans Act which mandates Area Agencies on Aging in every locality and, also, funds congregate dining programs, transportation, and information and referral services, as well as other direct service programs. These public programs are not only for the poor. Often funds are funneled to voluntary agencies, some of which are sectarian in nature (under the auspice of an ecumenical, interfaith, or special religious group or denomination) and others nonsectarian (such as the Red Cross). Proprietary (for-profit) counseling services can also be found in communities.

Public, voluntary, and for-profit medical care and mental health services also exist side by side. There are, for example, county nursing homes, sectarian homes for the aged, and proprietary nursing homes. There are, as well as Community Mental Health Centers, sectarian counseling services and peer counseling groups, and private clinical social workers, psychologists, and psychiatrists.

This bewildering array of services makes it difficult to understand the service network in any single community. Moreover, each organizaiton or individual that provides a service tends to do so separately, thus, services may exist uncoordinated with each other. Yet they are invaluable resources to church and synagogue. The challenge is to tap into these resources and to use and coordinate their offerings for the benefit of the elderly. It is obviously not possible for the religious sector to meet more than a small portion of the needs of the growing numbers of elderly persons in America. The religious sector, however, has an important and meaningful role because, among other reasons, it provides a caring

Chart 1-1
Three Groups of Elderly — 1986

	Well-Elderly Living in the Community (estimate = 80% of all elderly)	Severely Impaired Elderly Living in the Community (estimate 14% of all elderly)	Residents in Nursing Home (estimate = 6% of all elderly)
CHANGES OVER TIME			
The Aging Person	Retired couple, both in relatively good health	One or both develop a serious physical or mental impairment as health deteriorates	Health deteriorates significantly particularly after the death of a spouse, the living spouse enters a nursing home
	Both retain former levels of involvement in social and civic activities	Participation in community activities reduced and perhaps stops	
	Retain involvement in church/synagaogue, including regular attendance, at services	Church/synagogue attendance declines and perhaps stops	Participation in community and church/synagogue drop sharply, often totally stopping
Married Adult Children	Middle aged couple watching their children leave home	Adult children approaching retirement age or retired	Adult children retire. Usually they attempt to care for their parent for as long as possible but finally, overburdened, can not provide all the support needed
	Involvement in community activities such as employment, social and civic opportunities	Efforts are made to provide increasing support for impaired parents, perhaps even providing care in one adult child's home	
SUPPORT SERVICES NEEDED			
1. Health Care	Preventive care and maintenance of good health, increasing use of hospital	Home health care and intermittent hospital care needed	Institutional care in nursing home Intermittent hospital care needed
2. Mental Health Services	Counseling regarding retirement and use of leisure time, adjustment	Counseling for impaired elderly to adjust to impairments	Suport in adjusting to institutionalization

Chart 1-1 (continued)
Three Groups of Elderly

	Well-Elderly Living in the Community (estimate = 80% of all elderly)	Severely Impaired Elderly Living in the Community (estimate = 14% of all elderly)	Residents in Nursing Home (estimate = 6% of all elderly)
		Counseling, for spouse and family to provide support in caring for the impaired person	Counseling for family related to depression and institutionalizing a parent
3. In-home Services	Heavy home maintenance and repair work	Home maker, chore service, home maintenance and repair	Participation in programs sponsored by the home
4. Social Activities	Maintain participation in community, civic activities and church/synagogue, groups; join senior centers	Visitation, telephone reassurance, church and community participation as health permits	
5. Transportation	Assistance with general transportation	Specially adapted transportation system to provide assistance getting to the doctor and other essential activities, including church	Specially adapted transportation system to provide assistance getting to the doctor and other essential activities, including church
6. Housing	Private homes, senior citizens apartments, retirement housing	Adapted private home, sheltered care, congregate living facilities	24-hour institutional care
7. Religious Observances	Direct participation in church/synagogue	Private religious observances in the home, visitation, ministries for the homebound, attendance at church functions as health permits	Private religious observances, religious observance in the nursing home, visitation, special ministries for nursing home residents, attendance at church functions as health permits

community, a commitment to human wholeness and spiritual well-being, a set of churches and synagogues especially attuned to the needs of individuals and families, and an opportunity to work with and for the elderly in developing programs that fill critical gaps in services. Indeed, it is through working together with the secular sector that many of the unmet needs of the elderly can be addressed and filled.

Chapter Two

Spiritual Well-Being and Holistic Programs with the Elderly

A basic value is that each person is a unique individual. Therefore, to the greatest extent possible, each person must be allowed to express his or her uniqueness. To assure that programs facilitate the uniqueness of individuals, ministries must work with people, as well as for them. This is especially true for the elderly, who too often are made to feel dependent when they are fully able to make decisions that affect their lives. Thus, the elderly must be involved in every aspect of program development and implementation.

Beyond this common value, those who minister with and to the elderly will have their own particular personal values and theological beliefs. Although a concern for the welfare of others motivates all ministries, what we do for others is based on personal values and beliefs. It is sensible, therefore, to begin the development of any ministry with an exploration of the values that underlie the planned activities. For example, three individuals who are concerned about the welfare of residents of a nursing home may consider three very different kinds of programs. Ann, a Baptist, may immediately think of Bible study. Jim, a Unitarian, may suggest sharing the wisdom of his favorite philosophers. Sarah, an Orthodox

15

Jew, may wish to initiate a Sabbath study group on religious observances. All three concerned and committed individuals are interested in starting a group activity, but the content of each would be quite different because, in part, each reflects a different belief system.

Ministries with the elderly are developed for a variety of reasons, most often from a combination of biblical or theological inspiration, personal feelings, and an awareness of the needs of the seniors in the community. Authors (see, for example, Clements, 1981, and Clingan, 1980) have outlined many of the philosophical, biblical and theological reasons why there need to be ministries with the elderly, but, because of the limited focus of this book, we will not attempt to discuss the possible theologies of aging (see LeFevre and LeFevre, 1981, and Hiltner, 1975, for some perspectives). Rather, the purpose of this chapter is to outline the beliefs which shape our orientation to programming. This will be done by examining the implications of a holistic philosophy for the development of a perspective on the spiritual needs of older people and appropriate programs to serve those needs.

Holistic Concern for the Elderly

Two related ideas are central to our work: holism and spiritual well-being. The concept of holism is the older of the two. Many versions of this concept exist in the literature, and a holistic understanding of human nature can be traced back thousands of years. It has often been used as a response to other philosophies that were inclined to fragment human nature. Whether responding to the ancient Greeks' concept of a split between body and soul or the more recent reaction to the specialization in medicine, the concept of holism directs the practitioner to consider the total needs of the individual. Maimonides, a rabbi who lived in the twelfth century A.D., defined holism as the "affirmation of body, mind and spirit integrated in a whole, independent of and greater than the sum of its parts" (Ostrovsky, 1985, p. 64). This definition remains useful for us today. It suggests that, while several different aspects of human nature can be identified, it is important to understand these parts in relationship to all of the other aspects, in order to avoid fragmentation.

Although authors writing about holism agree that individuals are multidimensional, they often disagree when it comes to naming and counting the different dimensions. Most concur that there are physical, emotional, and social dimensions to a person. However, many authors, particularly social scientists, neglect the spiritual aspect of the person, and some prefer to subsume the spiritual under the psychological dimension. Our view is that it is useful to consider four different dimensions of the person: the physical, social, emotional, and spiritual.

4 dimensions of person-hood

Each of the four dimensions relates to an important portion of the individual. The physical relates to our bodies, without which we would not exist. The social refers to the part of the person that needs and relates to other persons. Few people can live happily alone. The emotional dimension is the expressive part of the person that relates to feelings. Often associated with laughter, crying and other emotions, this dimension is creative and responsive to the feelings of those persons around us. Finally, there is the spiritual dimension. Generally thought of as relating to God or to religion, this dimension is actually much more. It relates to the understanding that human beings are more than flesh, emotions, and thoughts. There is a spirit within us that can relate to that which is far greater than ourselves. The concept of holism also reaffirms that these four dimensions can not exist individually but only as an entity working together in some way.

spirituality maybe it's the combination of the other 3?

See p 18

Possibly one of the most difficult questions about holism is the matter of how the various dimensions relate to one another. At least three different views on this subject can be found. The first view is that each part is different and must be understood, assessed, and treated in its own right. Thus, to be overly simplistic, the surgeon should focus on what he or she can do best, such as the surgical removal of a ruptured appendix. If the person being operated on needs counseling, the surgeon often ignores this need or, at best, sends the patient to a counselor. The second view is that one dimension of the person is foundational to all others. Unless, for example, the physical aspect of the person is assured, it is needless to discuss such loftier portions of the person as the psychological or spiritual dimensions. Alternatively, if one looks at the spiritual as foundational, any intervention to assist someone would start with the spiritual dimension. In general, the intervention would always begin with the foundational piece and then look at its impact on the rest of the person. The third view is that one dimension unites the whole person by encompassing and permeating all parts of the person. This unifying dimension is difficult to distinguish from other aspects of the total person because it is part of each. This view is best exemplified in the work of the National Interfaith Coalition on Aging (NICA) as it defines the spiritual dimension of life. Thorson and Cook (1980) note, "the spiritual is not one dimension among many in life; rather it permeates and gives meaning to all life" (P Xiii).

In agreement with NICA, our view is that one dimension, the spiritual, permeates the others. In many ways this dimension is not distinguishable from the others because it is an important ingredient in each. The human spirit relates to our bodies, our minds, and our emotions, and it can influence our relationships with others, including our God. Our spirit is the common component which brings together our various parts. Numerous observers have noted individuals whose bodies have not been sick, but their spirit "had gone out of them," and they died. It is this spirit that helps us to integrate the parts of ourselves.

The Concept of Spiritual Well-Being

The concept of spiritual well-being is somewhat broader than many definitions of holism. Discussions of holism generally reflect the structure of the individual, whereas spiritual well-being considers both the structure of the individual *and* the relationship of the individual to his or her community and God. Although the concept of spiritual well-being is grounded in holism, it moves beyond internal needs to more fully acknowledge the environment and the relationship with God. This perspective on spiritual well-being became widely recognized when it appeared as one of the needs identified by the 1971 White House Conference on Aging. After much consultation and commentary, it was defined more specifically by the National Interfaith Coalition on Aging in 1975. The NICA definition of spiritual well-being states: "Spiritual well-being is the affirmation of life in a relationship with God, self, community and environment that nurtures and celebrates wholeness." This definition (from pages XIII and XIV of the Foreward to the book by Thorson and Cook, 1980) is explained by NICA as follows:

Spiritual Well-being is the Affirmation of Life

The spiritual is not one dimension among many in life; rather, it permeates and gives meaning to all life. The term spiritual well-being, therefore, indicates wholeness in contrast to fragmentation and isolation. "Spiritual" connotes our dependence on the source of life, God the Creator. — Holy spirit ! What, then, is spiritual well-being? We cannot regard well-being as equated solely with physical, psychological, or social good health. Rather, it is an affirmation of life. It is to say "Yes" to life in spite of negative circumstances. This is not mere optimism which denies some of life's realities; rather, it is the acknowledgement of the destiny of life. In the light of that destiny it is the love of one's own life and of the lives of others, together with concern for one's community, society, and the whole of creation, which is the dynamic of spiritual well-being. A person's affirmation of life is rooted in participating in a community of faith. In such a community one grows to accept the past, to be aware and alive in the present, and to live in hope of fulfillment.

A Relationship with God, Self, Community, and Environment

> Affirmation of life occurs within the context of one's relationship with God, self, community, and environment. God is seen as "Supreme Being," "Creator" of life, the Source and Power that wills well-being. All people are called upon to respond to God in love and obedience. Realizing we are God's children, we grow toward wholeness as individuals, and we are led to affirm our kinship with others in the community of faith, as well as the entire human family. Under God and as members of the community of faith, we are responsible for relating the resources of the environment to the well-being of all humanity.

That Nurtures and Celebrates Wholeness

> Human wholeness is never fully attained. Throughout life it is a possibility in process of becoming. In the Judeo-Christian tradition(s) life derives its significance through its relationship with God. This relationship awakens and nourishes the process of growth toward wholeness in self, crown moments of life with meaning, and extols the spiritual fulfillment and unity of the person.

The NICA definition of spiritual well-being has been helpful in reminding us that "wellness" must be understood in relation to the whole person. All of the parts of the person need to be considered, including his or her relationship with God, self, and community. More importantly this gives us a standard of well-being which is understood as a process of becoming a more balanced and well-integrated person, both internally and in relationship to the world around us.

A Life Span Perspective

relationships for old-age A holistic approach also necessitates a life span perspective. LeFevre (1984) has emphasized that the religious concern must be for "whole life span development, for what precedes old age as well as for the elderly" (page 1). There must be preparation for both the losses that characterize the latter part of life and for possible future growth in the later years of life. If growth is to occur, it will happen, according to LeFevre, through "the individual's sense that there is meaning in life" (page 3). The making of life meaningful to oneself is a life-long task that takes on different dimensions when age-associated losses occur and as the awareness of nonbeing becomes most real. Despite losses which may erode the possiblity of growth, there are changes which not only can sustain human dignity but also promote growth.

The sustaining of one's human dignity was noted in the previous chapter where we emphasized how the very old use reminiscence, as well as religious symbols and practices, to maintain a sense of the continuity of self. Beyond sustaining and maintaining oneself, and therefore one's sense of meaning to self and others, is the possibility for new meanings from a reassessment of one's life and goals and placing one's life in perspective in preparing for death (Erikson, 1950). The waning of our power toward the end of the life may actually facilitate a reassessment in which conventional values of mastery and control become of less importance; it may facilitate a realization of one's interdependence with others, of one's place in the continuity of generations, of one's uniqueness, and, possibly, a consciousness of making meaning of one's whole life (see, for example, Snyder, 1981).

Programming for the Whole Person

The concept of spiritual well-being has broad ramifications for the development of ministries with the elderly. Religious congregations often develop programs to address specific needs such as visitation programs, group activities, and clubs of various types. These programs are appropriately a part of the life of churches and synagogues. But, are they holistic in nature? Obviously, these programs are not designed to respond to all the needs of an individual. Yet, the important consideration is not whether a given activity focuses on recreational, spiritual, or physical concerns but whether it is open to encountering and ministering to other parts of the person. Thus, a church may provide a Bible study for its older members; but, if one of them becomes sick, someone should be able to help the individual obtain the necessary medical care.

A holistic ministry—whether it is in the community, a hospital, or a nursing home—must recognize the needs of the elderly, as well as the abilities of the social service agencies in the community to assist them. Clergy and lay persons, including the elderly, when ministering with seniors often encounter medical, emotional, or environmental needs that they are unable to address. Rather than assuming that nothing can be done, it may be helpful to add referrals to other community agencies to the list of available ministries. Conversely, social service and medical agencies need to be more responsive to the spiritual concerns of the elderly, referring them to an appropriate person, or persons, for assistance.

One of the dilemmas of holistic ministry is raised by the older person who tells his or her clergy or a lay person about a problem for which he or she does not wish to seek help from a community agency. For example, an elderly woman feels her husband is having an emotional problem but refuses to seek help from a mental health center. She may, however, turn to her minister, priest or rabbi. As teacher, preacher, and confidant, the clergy often find out about the problems of the members of the congregation but are unable to assist the individuals. When a doctor learns about a health problem, or a psychologist a mental health problem, it is generally because someone has sought help. However, clergy are different. They, for example, are more likely to live in the commuinty in which they serve (Naperstek, 1978) and are more likely to be viewed as a friend and neighbor. Thus, they often encounter concerns for which the individual is unwilling or unable to seek help. In these cases, the role of the concerned clergy or lay person should be to begin to help the individual to identify the need and the acceptability of help from an appropriate source.

Spiritual Well-being and Ministry with the Elderly

Concern for the quality of life has traditionally been a part of ministry, although the application of this concern has varied among denominations and local congregations. Development of ministries with the aged has raised questions such as, how should we minister to older people, should the elderly be included in the programs available to all members, or should they have separate programs, and when and how should seniors be involved in providing the services or programs for seniors? The answers to these and other similar questions generally depend on factors such as the availability of resources, as well as the underlying philosophical and theological consideratons of the congregation. However, the spiritual well-being of the seniors involved in these programs is also an important consideration in making decisions about the programs.

As noted at the beginning of this chapter, any consideration of spiritual well-being must take into account that elderly who receive services are, in effect, consumers, and they should be consulted as to the nature of the programs desired and involved in the planning and implementaton of such programs. Spiritual well-being is an individual experience. Too often, programs are developed for older people based on how younger people feel seniors could derive benefits. Consulting the elderly in question may confirm this, but it may also suggest other possibilities. An example of this is discussed by Malcolmson (1980) when he described his own work in pastoral visitation. Prior to the 1976 gas shortage, Reverend Malcolmson had an active home visitation ministry. However, when unable to visit during the gas shortage, he mailed a questionnaire to all of the parishioners who had been visited. Surprisingly, he found that "not every family demanded a visit: a few families did not even desire it.'' Such eye-opening experiences suggest that obtaining input from the seniors involved with a ministry can save both time and energy. Further, it provides a means for honoring the needs, concerns, personal history and, most importantly, the spiritual well-being of the individual senior.

Indeed, spiritual well-being requires an understanding of the elderly as whole persons. This includes honoring both the past and present lives of the older person. In fact, using memories of their past is one way of enhancing the present lives of an older person. Psychotherapists have developed therapeutic approaches using the inevitable life review of the old as a way to resolve life long conflicts (Butler, 1963) or to reaffirm identity (Grunes, 1981). Although, a common myth suggests that older persons spend too much time talking about the past, Butler suggests that this can be used as a therapeutic tool to be supportive of the individual. While change is unavoidable in the lives of seniors, supporting spiritual well-bing may involve at least understanding the importance of the past in shaping the present lives of older people. and younger ones, too!

Yet, an understanding of how the past has shaped individuals is insufficient. To enhance spiritual well-being, we must provide experiences that assure continuity in life. The unique role of church and synagogue, as well as religious practices, in assuring continuity and a personal sense of identity, can not be underestimated. With advancing age, losses are likely to occur, and it is the stability of their church and synagogue, and their religion, that gives many elderly the anchor they need to overcome loss and to still be themselves.

Conclusion

Holism and spiritual well-being of the elderly are more than abstractions. They provide us with criteria to determine whether or not we are enhancing the quality of life. Above all, each ministry must attend to the uniqueness of the individual, as well as to a concern for his or her contribution to the congregation and community. It should take seriously those aspects of each person's past that have contributed to the satisfaction of an individual life, as well as how we can reaffirm the uniqueness and identify of each individual through his or her participation in the religious community and in religious practices. Yet we must also strive to offer opportunities for growth and for continued contributions to life. For the elderly, as for all of us, our quality of life is enhanced as we strive toward a state of spiritual well-being and support others in this process.

Chapter Three

Church and Synagogue in Programming with the Aging

Church and synagogue are of immense importance to the elderly. Commenting on the importance of religious institutions, Palmore (1980) has written:

> Churches and synagogues deserve special consideraton because they are the single most pervasive community institution to which the elderly belong. All the other community institutions considered together, including senior citizen centers, clubs for elders, unions, etc., do not involve as many elders as churches and synagogues. (P. 236)

Palmore's observation is supported by information on the significance of religion in the lives of the elderly. More than four of five elderly (86 percent) believe in the existence of God (Riley and Foner, 1968). Similarly, a national poll showed that about three out of four of those age sixty and over report that religion is important in their lives (Harris, et al., 1975).

Church and synagogue attendance among the elderly further reflects the importance of religion in the lives of the elderly. The national poll also showed that four of five of those sixty-five and over had been to church or synagogue in the previous two weeks. However, for the old-old, attendance decreases. Some of the very old are too frail to attend services, while others do not have transportation or cannot climb the steps of the church or synagogue. There are some older people who say they "can't afford nice clothing" to go to services, and still others feel that younger members of the congregation have pushed them aside. Although attendance at formal worship decreases among the very old, personal religious practices, such as reading the Bible, prayer, and watching religious programs on television, are often maintained or even increased (Gray and Moberg, 1977).

Do these facts suggest people become more religious as they grow older? The evidence suggests that people maintain their religious beliefs. Indeed, Hunsberger (1985) found that elderly persons of high Christian Orthodoxy perceive themselves as becoming more religious from age ten on, whereas those of low Christian Orthodoxy perceive themselves as becoming slightly less religious. Certainly, those who perceive themselves to be religious must have opportunites to participate in church and synagogue. Moreover, there is evidence that religious beliefs, as well as church attendance and private practices, are associated with well-being among the elderly. Relationships among the three indicators of religiosity (attendance, private practices and self-ratings of religiosity) and well-being are not found in large scale studies using heterogeneous samples of elderly persons (Blazer and Palmore, 1976; Steinitz, 1980). When, however, the focus is on homogeneous groups of elderly, modest associations are found between religiosity and well-being (found by Hunsberger, 1985, who focused on Christians in Ontario, Canada; Heisel and Faulkner, 1982, on urban blacks; and Markides, 1983, on Mexican Americans).

Thus, the current elderly have been religious and have attended a church or synagogue throughout their lives. They desire to continue to do so as they become older. The quest in advanced aging to retain a sense of self when internal bodily changes and external losses occur suggests that not only may religious attachments become of even greater personal significance in providing continuity and a sense of sameness, but that these attachments enhance a sense of personal well-being. Moreover, the elderly can be helped to reaffirm their faith and religious identity through current religious activities that facilitate a reconstruction of their faith experiences. It is by getting in touch with one's early life that the individual is able to become comfortable with the continuity and wholeness of their life, possibly grow, and transcend losses. Thus, programs sponsored by churches and synagogues, as well as sectarian agencies, can have a special importance to our elderly.

The Nature of Church- and Synagogue-Sponsored Programs for Older People

In describing the church, Paul Maves (1960) observed that, in general, church activities can be divided into two categories: primary and secondary functions. He defined five primary functions which relate to the communication of belief systems and provision of opportunities to worship and express one's faith. Secondary functions of the church involve responding to the social needs of the congregation, including providing social services. Most churches and synagogues provide a mixture of programs addressing the spiritual, social, and survival needs of their congregants. It is important however, to recognize that churches and synagogues generally do not conceive of themselves as providers of social services. The church or synagogue is primarily a caring community which extends its concern to the well-being of its members, as well as others around them. In many ways, church and synagogue are extended families. They often provide for members out of a sense of obligation and concern for families. In this way, church and synagogue become part of what is referred to as the ''natural helping network'' which is made up of family, friends, and neighbors ready and willing to help each other when needed (Froland, et al., 1981).

As each church or synagogue struggles to define its mission, the unique combination of beliefs and preferences expressed by the congregation will shape its religious and social programming. The theological position of a church or synagogue, as well as its leadership and the makeup of the congregation, are all significant factors which affect the decision making by the congregation. Resources, both human and financial, are also important. Together, these contributing factors will determine the type and mix of programs offered by a church or synagogue. Even within the same denomination, the type and level of activity sponsored by each church or synagogue will vary, based on each congregation's understanding of doctrine and interpretation of its mission and purpose (Hutchenson, 1979).

Types of Church and Synagogue Sponsored Programs

Looking more specifically at the types of services provided for the elderly by churches and synagogues, there has been very little systematic research on this topic. Some authors have developed general summaries of the types of services available to the elderly through religious organizations, while others have discussed one or more model programs found in individual churches and synagogues with the intent of encouraging further program development. However, several noteworthy studies of church- and synagogue-sponsored programs for the elderly stand out. Steinitz (1981), in her intensive study of churches and synagogues in "Laketown," identified twelve general categories of church and synagogue sponsored programs for the elderly, including assurance of friendship, visitation, work opportunities, home personal health care, and social activities.

In a more extensive national survey of churches and synagogues, Cook (1976) identified fifty-two types of services provided for the elderly by church and synagogue groups, including supports provided at the national, regional, area, and local levels within the various religious structures. The services identified by Cook are quite specific in nature and include programs such as advocacy, counseling, day care, education, income maintenance, in-home services, nutrition services, retirement training, and transportation services. This study further revealed that, at the local or congregational level, churches and synagogues generally provided programs which included two to six distinct services to seniors, with a median number of three services offered by the local religious institutions in the survey.

Informal and Formal Programs

Not only do the types of programs vary from one church or synagogue to another, but the way that programs are organized also differs. At one extreme, we find many services that are provided on an informal basis; that is, spontaneously as they are needed. Transportation is an example of this kind of service when Mr. Albert, who needs a ride, simply calls his minister or another designated person in the congregation. Often this kind of assistance is on an intermittent basis and offered one time, several times, or indefinitely, but it stops once Mr. Albert's need no longer exists.

At the opposite extreme, we may find a religious organization that has highly structured and formalized programs. Using the transportation example again, we may find a church or synagogue with a formally organized bus system that runs a very specific route every week at a set time. The transportation service is widely advertised and runs on a regular schedule from week to week. The group of passengers using the bus may change, but the service continues. There are criteria which help the driver decide who should and should not use the bus. These criteria, for example, may limit ridership to older congregants who do not have alternative forms of transportation. The driver clearly would be specially trained not only to drive the bus but also to manage the people using the bus.

Formal and informal programs differ in many ways, but both have important places within the church and synagogue. On an informal basis, churches and synagogues can provide a wide variety of support services without a substantial investment of resources. Further, informal services can provide a very personalized response to an individual's needs. Formally organized services often require more resources but can make a service widely available to a large group of people on an equitable basis. Neither approach to organizing a program is particularly good or bad, simply a different way of structuring a program. While it is often difficult to know how to place programs of varying structure along a continuum, the extremes are designated as formal and informal program.

Four Roles in Serving the Elderly

In our investigation into the role of religious institutions in the aging network, we have found that the services provided by churches and synagogues fall into four basic groups. Each of these service groups suggests a role for the church and synagogue in serving older people. These groups are:

    I. Providing religious programs,

    II. Serving as a host,

    III. Providing pastoral care programs, and

    IV. Providing social services.

The services falling into any one of these categories can be organized in an informal or formal manner. Some of the programs are led by trained professionals, while others are not. Indeed, many of the people doing the actual work in these programs were not clergy or other professionals but lay people, including older adults themselves.

ROLE I: PROVIDING RELIGIOUS PROGRAMS. The category of religious programs includes the type of activities that one would most likely anticipate being provided by a church or synagogue. This includes the midweek and weekend worship services that are held in a majority of churches and synagogues. Other types of religious programs include special worship services for seniors, religious study groups, prayer groups, and holiday remembrances, such as special programs and food baskets. Further, many churches and synagogues provide services which facilitate participation in church- and synagogue-sponsored activities. Transportation to activities is an obvious example of this type of support. Some religious institutions also provide ramps, large print reading materials, and hearing aids to encourage participation in activities by seniors with physical handicaps. For the religious older person, religious programs are extremely important and need to be considered as much a priority as any other type of program.

ROLE II: SERVING AS A HOST. Particularly since the 1972 Amendment to the Older Americans Act, churches and synagogues have become hosts to numerous social service activities. Possibly the most common of these are the meals programs. It is not unusual to find the social service agencies providing some of their lunch programs in the basements of local churches or synagogues. In recent years, religious organizations have become conscious of the fact that their buildings often stand empty during the week, seeing their greatest use on weekends. To make better use of the space, other community groups, including social service agencies, are allowed to sponsor activities in these buildings. The church or synagogue itself generally does not assume responsibility for organizing or managing these programs. Program participants may or may not include members of the congregation. In effect, the agency is simply borrowing the space in the building to provide a service.

ROLE III. PROVIDING PASTORAL CARE SERVICES. The next group refers to the pastoral care services available in churches and synagogues. These services can be provided for individuals, families, or groups. They are generally directed toward the members of the congregation and are a part of the general life of the congregation. The services for individuals can include visitation to seniors who are homebound, hospitalized, or nursing home residents; telephone reassurance; home delivered meals; and assistance with housekeeping. They can also include general transportation, food distribution programs, and free clothing. As a general rule, clergy and lay leaders (including older adults) provide these services as they are needed. Were clergy and lay leaders to receive a large number of such requests in any given month, they probably would not be able to respond to all of them.

Pastoral care services can also be developed for groups. Many educational activities, discussion groups, and various types of social activities can be considered pastoral care services. This may also include some types of support groups and self-help groups. The focus of these group activities may or may not include what could be called "religious concerns," and some advertising may be done to attract participants from the community. There is generally no fee for services provided in these groups. Many of these groups do not even have a leader specifically trained to work with the group. While called pastoral care services, this group of activities moves the church or synagogue much closer to providing the type of services usually sponsored by social agencies. However, they are still not considered to be social services, by either the church or synagogue or the participants in the programs.

Now becoming more common in congregations is peer counseling: counseling, that is, by peers who are trained to do so. Indeed, elderly peer counselors can make invaluable contributions to other seniors. Sometimes the counseling focuses on specific issues, such as legal or financial issues, but it can be much broader and include counseling on emotional issues. A variant of peer counseling is self-help groups such as widow-to-widow groups where, through the sharing of experiences, middle-aged and older persons find comfort and are able to successfully re-engage in life.

Pastoral care services in church and synagogue often respond as would a friend or neighbor. Because these services are often provided spontaneously when a request is made, they are generally considered to be informal services. When the need or interest in the service subsides, the service is usually discontinued. However, it must be pointed out that some of these pastoral care services can be more formally organized.

ROLE IV: PROVIDING SOCIAL SERVICES. At times, a church or synagogue may choose to develop a formal social service program in response to a need in its community. Generally this type of program is developed in response to a "gap" in the local network of services. The gap may exist because there is a need in the community but no organized program which addresses the need. For example, there may be a need for inexpensive, in-home supports for older people but very few low-cost home companion or housekeeping services available. A church or synagogue may then develop these types of services. Alternatively, services may exist in the community but may not adhere to a value system supported by the church or synagogue. In this case, the religious institution may become involved in developing a service which is provided in a manner that is consistent with its belief system. Sectarian nursing homes, retirement centers, and senior clubs are all examples of this type of service.

In contrast to pastoral care services, these social services tend to be much more formally organized and permanently structured. When clergy become aware of the fact that many families in the community have inadequate food, several types of responses can be developed. On one level, he or she may choose to provide a bag of groceries to families when they request help. This is clearly a pastoral care service. On another level, a group of clergy may work with others to develop a food pantry which provides food to community residents meeting defined eligibility criteria. This pantry would be staffed by someone who knows the basic eligibility criteria, screens applicants, and provides food to eligible individuals. While this service may be provided with the same motive as the pastoral care service, the differences in attitude and structure make it a formal social service program rather than a pastoral care service. Both the church or synagogue and the program participants would identify this type of program as a service program.

Working Together

When developing a program, a church or synagogue has three strategies that can be used to create this new service. One choice is to work independently to develop this service. This gives considerable freedom and autonomy but means that the church or synagogue must rely on developing its own expertise and resources without ongoing support from others. A second strategy would be to initiate an ecumenical or interfaith effort, joining together a group of churches and synagogues willing to work toward the same goals. Finally, a church or synagogue may choose to work with one or more social service agencies to develop a new program. Either a single church or synagogue, or an ecumenical/interfaith group may come together with the social service agencies. Regardless of the content of the new program, any one of these three strategies may be used to begin developing the new program.

While each strategy has its strengths, it is our belief that working together in program development is extremely important. Ecumenical or interfaith efforts between groups of churches and synagogues, as well as combined efforts among churches, synagogues, and social service agencies can yield many benefits. These benefits may include an opportunity to develop a broad understanding of the needs of older people and gaps within the current service system; the sharing of information about current services; the sharing of expertise on program development; the sharing of resources needed for the new program, and possibility of using resources to develop the best possible set of services for older people; an opportunity to work together to refine and improve the current network of services; the chance to encourage better interaction between existing service providers, including making referrals to each other when appropriate; and an opportunity to develop a broad view of services which discourages unnecessary duplication of services.

Beyond these benefits, it is possible that working together can provide a holistic approach to ministry with the elderly. With few exceptions, churches and synagogues cannot single-handedly develop an entire set of services which meet all the needs of older people. Yet, the church or synagogue must be prepared to respond to the physical, psychological, social, and spiritual needs of the individuals whom they serve, if they are to honor the whole person. By working together, it is possible to coordinate services in a manner that can meet the needs of the whole individual. To insure this, the church or synagogue does not need to provide all types of services but must know about the services available within the community. By making referrals, an appropriate package of needed services can be coordinated for an individual.

Chapter Four

Community Church: An Example of Decision Making in Action

As we consider the ways churches and synagogues can respond to the need and concerns of the elderly, it may be helpful to offer a concrete example. Community Church is not a specific institution; rather it is a composite of the many churches and synagogues which labor to be congregations in the changing world. Like all churches and synagogues, the composite church reflects many influences including its theology, leadership, membership, and community context. Community Church is not, however, a prototypic church. It has simply been constructed to capture many of the common struggles, concerns and successes when church and synagogue attempt to develop programs with the elderly.

Community Church

Community Church is an average-sized, nondenominational church. In common with many other congregations, about 20 percent of Community Church's membership is over the age of sixty-five, almost twice the percentage of seniors in the general metropolitan area. Many of the older members were part of the original group of families that started the congregation.

Community Church has one minister, Reverend Henry, who is supported in his work by other part-time and volunteer staff members. The church has two primary decision-making groups, a board of elders and a board of deacons. As with many other churches, the deacons traditionally have been responsible for the church's efforts to serve the elderly.

Numerous social and management problems cross Reverend Henry's desk on any given day. The youth of the neighborhood are becoming involved with alcohol and drugs; the other churches in his neighborhood are pressuring him to support a petition to end the latest war; attendance at church is down; and if someone doesn't repair the church's steeple, it is likely to break off. Somewhere, amid the noise and clutter of paper, petitions, telephone calls, and sermon plans, is a competent pastor who is doing a responsible job of discharging his office. Yet Reverend Henry is also aware of the many things that he had not been able to do. On this list he often finds the needs and concerns of the elderly. About four years ago, Reverend Henry tried to persuade the board of elders to help him look into utilizing the fellowship hall for a hot lunch program for seniors. In response to this proposal, he was told by the older members of the board that this was not needed and asked if he would please concentrate on attracting more young people to the church. Reverend Henry was puzzled by this response but complied with the request.

Recently, Reverend Henry has again been confronted with the needs of the elderly by Mrs. Brown. Mrs. Brown is a relatively new member of the congregation who has been active in churches all of her life. She was elected to the board of elders during the last election. Mrs. Brown talked with Reverend Henry several weeks prior to her election about her own aged mother who was becoming progressively more forgetful and, at times, even angry and combative. Mrs. Brown and her two sisters have been taking turns having their mother stay with them since their father died over a year ago.

Maybe best for programs to come from cong. See 41 + 48

Inspired by an article in the local newspaper about the horrendous treatment of the elderly in nursing homes, as well as by her own struggles, Mrs. Brown decided that her church should do more for the elderly. Her initial effort to gain support in this endeavor was talk to Reverend Henry. Reverend Henry explained that the needs of the elderly were already being addressed in several ways. He noted that visitation to shut-in congregants is done by the board of deacons. The deacons make visits to local nursing homes at Christmas, Easter, and other occasions as time permits. The ladies in the women's club also visit older people from time to time, and they assume responsibility for the annual Christmas basket project. Of course Reverend Henry also visits those persons he feels could benefit from having him stop by, as well as anyone who is in the hospital.

Reverend Henry futher noted that any elderly person who needed a ride to church, or any other such assistance, could call him. He makes arrangements to meet these needs as they arise, although he observed that he receives very few calls of this type. Finally, he mentioned his effort to gain approval for the use of the fellowship hall at the church for a meal program for the elderly and the fact that his efforts had been thwarted by the older members of the board. He suggested, however, that times had changed, and, if Mrs. Brown were interested in following through her ideas, she should discuss them with the board of elders.

Community Church Develops a Program

Mrs. Brown raised her concerns with the board of elders at their next meeting. Their reception was polite and resulted in the suggestion that a joint committee on the needs of the elderly could be developed utilizing the energies of Mrs. Brown from their board and one or two people from the board of deacons. With some help from Reverend Henry and consultation with the board of deacons, a committee of three was set up to investigate the needs of the elderly. Serving with Mrs. Brown on the new Seniors Committee was a senior citizen, who was also in charge of visitation, and a social worker. The committee turned out to be well-chosen because their combined talents and experience enabled them to develop a set of services using a well-conceived planning process.

Following a conversation with Reverend Henry, the new Seniors Committee concluded that the first step in planning was to try to determine what services were needed by the elderly. In an effort to begin to understand the concerns of older congregants, the committee decided to embark on two tasks: (1) to survey older members of the congregation to identify needs as perceived by the elderly themselves; and (2) to initiate discussions with local social services agencies to better understand what services for the elderly existed in the community.

The initial discussion of the survey of needs (usually referred to as a needs assessment survey) was disastrous. One member of the Senior Committee demanded a highly personalized approach in which each elderly member of the congregation was asked directly, in person, about his or her needs and wishes. An open meeting was suggested as an alternative but all quickly agreed that the most needy might not attend and also that the most outspoken would most likely be those with the least amount of need. It can indeed be quite embarrassing to discuss personal needs in public. Other alternatives were suggested: a telephone interview; a questionnaire of modest length that could be filled out at home and mailed in and a simple post card survey. Now at an impasse, the committee decided to invite a young member of the congregation, a sociologist at a local college, to attend the next meeting and to advise them.

At the next meeting, Dr. Evans joined the Committee and discussed some of the general kinds of questions that must be addressed before deciding the final way of gathering information. Are there resources for face-to-face interviews? Either the members of the Committee would have to devote a great deal of their own time or they would need to pay interviewers. They could, however, interview a smaller number (a representative or random sample of older congregants) but this procedure could defeat the overall purpose of mounting a total congregation effort. If, in turn, they wished the whole congregation involved, they could design a questionnaire for younger, as well as older, members of the congregation. To decide who should be surveyed and how they should be surveyed, Dr. Evans said it was necessary to consider how the information would be analyzed so that a report could be written. The simpler the questions and answers, the easier and less biased the analysis. Team members then asked Dr. Evans to discuss a self-administered questionnaire that would be mailed back. The following is a summary of his remarks.

Any time that a mail-in questionnaire is developed, there is that sinking feeling that, after all the work of developing and preparing it for distribution, no one will return it. There are ways, however, of increasing the return rate. For example, the inclusion of an addressed return envelope saves the recipient the trouble of determining where to send the questionnaire. The questionnaire should be kept as brief as possible with four pages the maximum length. To ensure that it falls within this length, it can be typed on legal-sized paper. Be sure that the questionnaire begins with an introduction as to its purpose and how to fill it out. Instructions for each question must be clear. Try it out on yourselves or others to make sure every question is asked clearly and that instructions are understandable. Review each question carefully and consider the pros and cons of using a "fixed-choice" or "open-ended" format where the respondent answers in his or her own words. If a fixed-choice format is used, request the respondent to either "check only one" or "check as many as apply" Fixed-choice questions are easier to analyze, but open-ended questions allow respondents to give their own input. Try to use as many fixed-choice questions as possible, but also include some open-ended questions.

It is necessary to consider whether or not to keep the individual responses to questions confidential. Most researchers agree that ensuring confidentiality will increase the number of questionnaires returned, as well as increasing the candor and honesty of the respondent. Confidentiality can be ensured by not requesting the name of the respondent. However, even instruments that do not request a name can have their confidentiality violated if they require the respondent to hand the questionnaire directly to the pastor or a member of the committee. While confidentiality can enhance the response rate, it may not be appropriate if the respondent is asked whether he or she wishes to contribute to the effort. It does very little good to ask respondents what they would be willing to contribute, if they do not identify themselves. The questionnaire can remain confidential, however, by including a separate postcard on which offers to contribute can be recorded. Thus they can contribute to the ministry by returning the postcard while maintaining confidentiality of the questionnaire.

When Dr. Evans completed his presentation, a lively discussion ensued regarding pros and cons of a self-administered questionnaire mailed to all elderly members of community church. By this time, the lone committee member who had vehemently insisted on face-to-face personalized interviews recognized the enormous personal cost in time of committee members undertaking the interview, as well as the lack of funds to hire interviewers, and, moreover, the difficulty they would have in analyzing the information (data) if questions were not asked in the same way of all respondents. In turn, a self-administered questionnaire was attractive to the group, such as the one developed by the Church as Service Provider team at the University of Chicago (see appendix to this chapter). Yet several concerns were voiced regarding this kind of questionnaire. Many elderly members of the congregation have difficulty holding a pencil because of arthritis, others have poor vision, and still others will not have the patience or take the time to fill out the questionnaire. A low response rate, they agreed, could be a real possibility. Finally, neither they nor Dr. Evans had the resources to either analyze responses by hand or by computer. Thus the committee decided to do a postcard survey (see Clingan, 1980, for an example).

All elderly congregants (in this instance, sixty years of age and over) were then mailed a prepaid postcard requesting a listing on the card of unmet needs. Included was a cover letter detailing the purpose of the survey.

The postcards that were returned suggested unmet needs for police protection and a range of social services. Although the elderly are not physically assaulted more often than persons of other age groups, they are likely to be injured more seriously if assaulted. Being knocked down could result in a bruise for a young person but a broken hip for an elderly person. This concern was referred to Reverend Henry who has been having frequent discussions with police and other law enforcement groups about use of alcohol and drugs by adolescents.

Concern about the lack of social services was discussed with personnel from the several local social service agencies. To the surprise of the committee, these personnel were convinced that most of the kinds of services identified already existed in the community. Although local social service agencies did not always have adequate resources to serve those with special needs, apparently there was a fairly complete range of services offered through programs sponsored by federal, state, and local governments, along with voluntary and proprietary agencies. Thus, the committee determined that the first need they would address was to help the elderly and their families better understand and utilize the existing services. A specific problem identified by the committee was the lack of adequate support for families who were providing care for confused elderly in their own homes. These families had many unmet needs for help in the home and for emotional support.

Having identified these service needs, the Committee reported back to the church boards to gain approval for developing projects. Additionally, the Committee decided to talk with other local churches to see if they would be interested in joining them in their efforts. After these discussions, several churches of different denominations, as well as synagogues, designated representatives to be part of an ecumenical group to address the unmet needs of the elderly in the community. Several interested social service agencies also sent representatives to join the committee. Recognizing the advantage of their greater resources and their expanded access to the elderly, this combined committee worked to establish a "common vision" which could be used to shape new program initiatives. To provide this common vision, they worked together to answer the following questions about each of their proposed projects.

1. What is the purpose of the new project? What specific services will be provided?

2. Who is going to be served by this program? Will it be designed to serve all elderly or specific subgroups within the elderly population? Will families be included? Will other nonelderly be included among those served by this program?

3. How will the program be structured? Will it be formal or informal?

4. Who will implement this program? Who will provide the necessary labor or put it together? Can the recipients contribute something to it?

5. Where will the program be set up? What type of physical space is needed?

6. What resources will be needed to provide such a program? What types of equipment, supplies, staffing, money, and so on will be necessary? Does the committee have access to sufficient resources to support the program?

7. What does the committee hope will be accomplished by this program? What outcomes should be expected after all of its labors?

8. How will the group know if it has accomplished its goals? How will it evaluate whether or not the program was a success? What evaluation strategies should be used?

9. What is the time table for beginning this new program? What sequence of activities must be completed to start the program? How does this fit into other planned activities in the churches and community-at-large?

After considering these questions, the ecumenical planning group developed the following goals and tasks.

Goal: Enhance the knowledge of elderly and lay visitors of the existing human services.

1. Hold a services fair on weekday morning. Allow each participating social service agency to have a table at which its representatives can talk to seniors, lay visitors, and clergy about their programs.

2. Obtain ongoing news from local social service agencies to be printed in church bulletin inserts and church newsletters.

Goal: Assist clergy and lay visitors (including older adults) to better understand how to properly make referrals to social service agnecies.

Tasks:

1. Hold a workshop in cooperation with the local social service agencies to discuss referral processes.

2. Create a directory of services which lists both local services and contact persons.

Goal: Develop supports for families caring for confused elderly at home.

Tasks:

1. Establish an ongoing support group made up of families caring for confused elderly at home.

2. Develop a respite program which provides people who are able to go into the home and care for the confused elderly, giving families periodic breaks from this responsibility.

Beyond defining their goals and tasks, the group attempted to specify processes for implementing the programs. This involved answering questions 3 through 9 on the foregoing list, which clarified exactly how the program would be organized, led, and evaluated. As a result of this process, the planning group was able to work with neighborhood churches, synagogues and social service agencies to achieve its goals. It took this group two years to accomplish its initial goals and during this time new ideas and more goals were added, yielding an ongoing process of planning and developing needed programs for the elderly. Regular evaluations were particularly helpful in assessing the success of the new initiatives as well as for refining goals and identifying new needs.

Discussion of Community Church

The program development process by Community Church shares several facets with processes observed in many other churches. Prior to Mrs. Brown's involvement at Community Church, for example, Reverend Henry had approached his church board with the suggestion of using the fellowship hall for a hot meal program for the elderly, only to discover that the elderly board members themselves did not perceive this as a priority for the church. Yet, the postcard survey suggested that a hot meal program could benefit many elderly. Unfortunately, many elderly individuals on church boards are the most active and healthy among the elderly; that is, young-old persons who do not completely recognize the needs of the old-old. The well elderly are not likely to adequately represent sick and shut-in elderly who can not be as active in the life of the church. Because Reverend Henry did not ask those persons who might have needed the hot meals program but, instead, listened to those who did not need the service, a potentially valuable ministry opportunity was missed.

Similar to other church and synagogue programs was the initiation by a lay person. In some organizations, professionals must be at the center of every activity. In churches and synagogues, however, most activities are led by the laity (including older adults). Indeed, Steinitz (1981) found that social service programs in churches and synagogues are generally designed by and for lay congregants. Although the role of the clergy in programming for and with the elderly will vary from one congregation to another, it is generally considered a positive reflection on the clergy to have these programs in the hands of the laity.

As portrayed in our example, the motivating force for developing the new programs came from the needs of a single congregant. Indeed, it takes at least one person to become sensitive to the needs of the elderly, to speak up, and then to initiate action. Although generally very positive, if the motivation is based on a personal problem (in our example, Mrs. Brown's difficulties with her elderly mother), it is necessary that this person's problems do not adversely affect the project. It is certainly helpful for someone who is struggling with a personal problem to share the problem with others. The problems of caring for a mother, however, may not be everyone's problem. Mrs. Brown as well as the rest of the committee must be cautioned, for example, that not all elderly are like her mother, and the needs of other elderly may be quite different. Certainly, it may be healthy for Mrs. Brown to become knowledgeable about other elderly because she can gain a better perspective on her own parent. But it can also be problemmatic.

Possibly our example is dissimilar from other churches or synagogues because we presented a very systematic and successful planning and implementation process. Clearly, our intent was to offer a more ideal process. Many religious organizations do, however, use elements of this general planning process as they develop programs (Worley, 1978). Further, any church or synagogue can begin with the basic planning strategy suggested in our example and modify it for its own use. If the basic decision-making process were to be extracted from our example, it would yield a series of questions which are summarized on Chart 4-1. The process of answering these questions allows every member of a planning committee to see what is happening and understand what needs to be done, what was referred to earlier as a common vision for the new ministry.

A number of important principles in developing new programs were illustrated in the planning process used by Community Church and the ecumenical group. These principles can be used as guides as groups embark on the planning process and struggle to answer the key questions which have just been outlined. Among the most important of these principles are the following: goto p52

Chart 4–1
Decision in Program Development

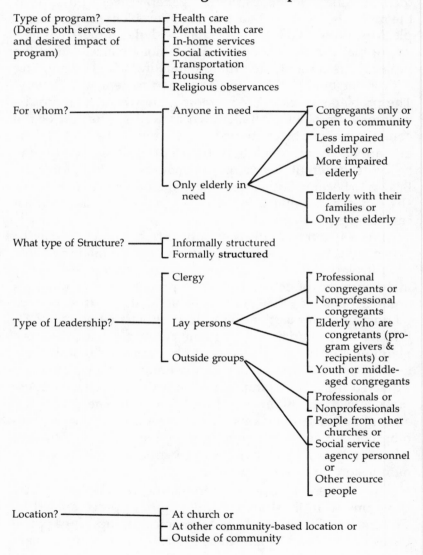

Type of program? —————————— ⌐ Health care
(Define both services   ⊢ Mental health care
and desired impact of   ⊢ In-home services
program)   ⊢ Social activities
                          ⊢ Transportation
                          ⊢ Housing
                          ⌊ Religious observances

For whom? ——————————— ⌐ Anyone in need ———————— ⌐ Congregants only or
                                               ⌊ open to community

                                               ⌐ Less impaired
                                                 elderly or
                                                 More impaired
                                                 ⌊ elderly
                           ⌊ Only elderly in ⟨
                               need   ⌐ Elderly with their
                                                 families or
                                                 ⌊ Only the elderly

What type of Structure? ———— ⌐ Informally structured
                                   ⌊ Formally **structured**

                                 ⌐ Clergy   ⌐ Professional
                                                           congregants or
                                                     ⌊ Nonprofessional
                                                          congregants
Type of Leadership? ———————— ⊢ Lay persons ⟨   ⌐ Elderly who are
                                                             congretants (pro-
                                                             gram givers &
                                                             recipients) or
                                   ⌊ Outside groups   ⌊ Youth or middle-
                                                             aged congregants

                                               ⌐ Professionals or
                                               ⌊ Nonprofessionals
                                               ⌐ People from other
                                                 churches or
                                               ⊢ Social service
                                                 agency personnel
                                                 or
                                               Other reource
                                               ⌊ people

Location? ———————————————— ⌐ At church or
                                   ⊢ At other community-based location or
                                   ⌊ Outside of community

Chart 4–1 (continued)
Decision in Program Development

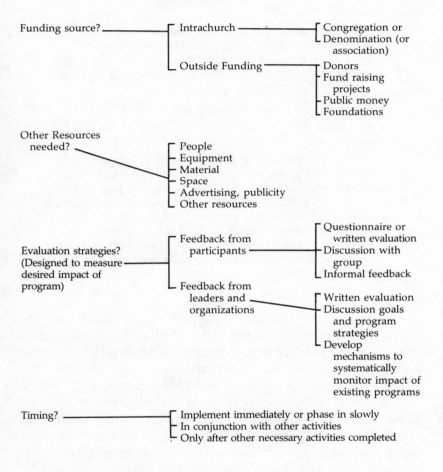

Funding source? —— Intrachurch ——— Congregation or
 Denomination (or
 association)

 Outside Funding —— Donors
 Fund raising
 projects
 Public money
 Foundations

Other Resources
 needed? —— People
 Equipment
 Material
 Space
 Advertising, publicity
 Other resources

Evaluation strategies?
(Designed to measure
desired impact of
program) —— Feedback from
 participants ——— Questionnaire or
 written evaluation
 Discussion with
 group
 Informal feedback

 Feedback from
 leaders and
 organizations —— Written evaluation
 Discussion goals
 and program
 strategies
 Develop
 mechanisms to
 systematically
 monitor impact of
 existing programs

Timing? —— Implement immediately or phase in slowly
 In conjunction with other activities
 Only after other necessary activities completed

1. Work directly with the elderly who will be served to identify needs and preferred programmatic responses.

2. Develop a program that can be adequately supported with available resources. Consider the possibilities of working with other community groups, particularly if substantial resources are needed to develop the program.

3. Plan programs which enrich services and add to the diversity of options available to the elderly. Avoid unnecessary duplication of services. Maintain flexibility and sensitivity to the specialized needs of seniors whenever possible.

4. Try to build active planning and leadership roles for the older people who are to be served by the program.

5. Strive to maintain a holistic focus in programming. While a program may be designed primarily to meet a single need, realize that the whole person is being served and that many different types of needs can be addressed in a single program. Try to understand the physical, psychological, social and spiritual background of each older person you work with and strive to adjust programs to that person's unique set of needs and abilities.

Central to the concept of planning suggested in our example is a collaborative approach. Program development in any setting can be a complex process. When it includes representatives of more than one community group, however, the process becomes even more complex because each group may have a different view of what the program should address and how it should be carried out. Another issue is that the individual representatives of each institution may not have previously known each other. Thus the difficulties involved in getting to know and trust each other in a committee setting will be present. A consensus must be developed. Too often, we state that our purpose is to plan for something, like a community social services fair, assuming that everyone knows what this means and agrees on what needs to be done. This may not be the case. It is important for the group to take the time to understand each other, to plan together

and gain the input of each member of the planning committee. Although a collaborative approach is not always essential, there are a number of circumstances in which it is a very
effective strategy including the following situations: when
the number of persons in the congregation with a specific
need is not large enough to justify creation of a program, but
the need for the program exists for elderly throughout the
community; when the need for a program or service is clear,
yet no single congregation or community group has the
resources to develop it alone; when the creativity and expertise of two or more groups can be brought together to
enhance a service or program; and any time that new ideas,
different concepts, or an ecumenical perspective can be
brought together to enhance the service or program.

It is our belief that most programs and services can be
enhanced by working with other churches, synagogues, or
social service agencies. In the case of Community Church,
they could not have developed all of the suggested programs
alone. They had neither the resources nor the personnel to
sponsor these programs yet, by working with others, it was
possible to make these services available to seniors. Their
program was ultimately enhanced by cooperation with the
other churches and synagogues, as their ideas and resources
grew beyond the original vision. Further discussion of the
uses of collaboration will be discussed in Chapter 9 and 10.

APPENDIX A

Information about yourself

1. How often do you attend church/synagogue?
   _____ Regularly
   _____ Every once in a while
   _____ Not very much
   _____ Not at all

2. Do you wish that you could attend more?
   _____ No
   _____ Yes

2a.   If yes, what problems have you encountered that pre-
vent you from attending more often? Check all that
apply.
_____ I am too sick to attend
_____ I have a hard time climbing the stairs
_____ I can't hear the service
_____ I have trouble finding transportation
_____ My family is no longer available to go with me
_____ The services are too long for me to sit through
_____ I can't leave my spouse since he/she became ill
_____ Other: (Please explain): _____
_____

3.   How long have you been a member of the church/synagogue?
_____ All of my life
_____ More than 30 years
_____ 15 to 29 years
_____ 5 to 14 years
_____ 1 to 4 years
_____ I just joined the church
_____ I am not a member of the church

4.   Do you attend any church/synagogue functions other than
Sabbath worship?
_____ No
_____ Yes

4a.   If yes which ones? (Please include any religious func-
tions that are not actually taking place in the
church/synagogue.) Check as many of the following
items that you feel are appropriate.
_____ Men's or Women's group
_____ Adult Sunday School
_____ Bible Study
_____ A Golden Age Club or Center
_____ A city lunch program
_____ Choir
_____ Missions project
_____ Special projects (identify specific projects)
_____ Other: (Please specify): _____
_____

5. Please tell us about your living situation.
    _____ I live alone
    _____ I live with my husband or wife
    _____ I live with my brother, sister, or parent
    _____ I live with my children
    _____ I live with nonrelatives (friends, etc.)

6. Please tell us where you live.
    _____ I live in an apartment
    _____ I live in a condominium
    _____ I live in a mobile home
    _____ I live in a single family house
    _____ I live in a town house

    [handwritten: By choice or necessity? Rather be elsewhere? Why?]

7. Please tell us about your marital status.
    _____ I am married
    _____ I have never been married
    _____ I am divorced
    _____ I am widowed

8. Please tell us about your current employment status.
    _____ I am retired
    _____ I am semiretired
    _____ I am employed part-time
    _____ I am employed full time
    _____ I am involved in volunteer efforts

9. Do you drive a car?
    _____ No
    _____ Yes

    9a. If yes, do you own a car?
         _____ No
         _____ Yes

10. Do you live within walking distance of the church?
    _____ No
    _____ Yes

11. Do you have any health problems that you feel would limit
    your ability to participate in church/synagogue activities?
    _____ No
    _____ Yes

    11a. If yes, please specify: _____
    _____

Information about your needs

(Instruction set: The questions that follow are not intended to intrude into your personal affairs. Rather, they are to help us understand the general needs of the older members of the congregation in order to develop appropriate programs. Thus, for example, if we find that several people are having legal problems, we might be able to start a legal aid program.)

1.   Financial needs. Would you find it helpful to have information about any of the following? (Check all that apply.)
     _____ Social Security
     _____ Tax information
     _____ Investment
     _____ Insurance

2.   Legal needs. Would you find it useful to have any of the following available through the church? (Check all that apply.)
     _____ Information about protection from fraud
     _____ Information on wills
     _____ Information on guardianship
     _____ Information on how to find a lawyer that you can trust
     _____ Information or assistance paying for legal assistance

3.   Health needs. Do you feel that you could benefit from any of the following? (Check all that apply.)
     _____ Blood pressure checks
     _____ Routine blood tests
     _____ Nursing services at home
     _____ Nutrition information
     _____ Help selecting a doctor that you can trust
     _____ Information about medications

4.   Emotional health needs. Do you feel that you, or any one that you know could benefit from any of the following? (Check all that apply.)
     _____ Help finding a counselor that you can trust
     _____ Help for a problem with alcohol
     _____ Help for a constant feeling of depression
     _____ Help adjusting to widowhood
     _____ Help with family problems

5. Personal needs. Do you feel that you could benefit from any of the following? (Check all that apply.)
    _____ Help choosing a nursing home
    _____ Help preplanning a funeral
    _____ Pastoral visits
    _____ Communion at home
    _____ Other: Please be specific: _____
    _____

6. Help around the house. Do you ever need any of the following? (Check all that apply.)
    _____ Mowing the lawn
    _____ Snow removal
    _____ Help around the house
    _____ Other: Please specify: _____
    _____

7. Employment needs. Do you ever need any of the following? (Check all that apply.)
    _____ Help finding a job
    _____ Help finding volunteer opportunities

8. Recreation needs. Please tell us about the things that you enjoy doing.
    I enjoy _____
    I would like to learn to _____

Information about local social services

1. Have you ever used or been involved with any local social services?
    _____ No
    _____ Yes

    1a. If yes, which one(s) _____
    _____

    1b. If yes, did the agency meet your needs?
         _____ Yes
         _____ No   If no, what should they have done? _____
    _____

2.   Do you feel that your community has all of the social services that are needed by you and the other seniors that you know?
        _____ Yes
        _____ No

        2a.   If no, what services do you feel are missing? Please specify: _____
        _____

3.   Do you feel that there are some social services that the church should not be involved in?
        _____ No
        _____ Yes

        3a.   If yes, which ones? _____

Information about things that you would like to do

1.   Would you like to do more to help others?
        _____ No
        _____ Yes

        1a.   If yes, is there some reason why you are not able to do so?
        _____ No
        _____ Yes

2.   Are there specific services that you would like to give?
        _____ No
        _____ Yes

        2a.   If yes, What? _____

Information to focus congregational action

1.   How could the congregation better help you? _____
        _____

2.   Are you aware of any neighbors or friends of any age who need help? How do you think that the church/synagogue could help? _____
        _____

3.   What are your concerns for your future? _____

       _____

       _____

4.   What other suggestions do you have to help your congregation to be aware of aging persons' opportunities and needs? (Please do not hesitate to write on the back of the page.)

       _____

       _____

       _____

       _____

Thank you for your time, effort, and cooperation. Please send this questionnaire to the church/synagogue or bring it when you come to services or to a meeting.

Part II

Serving Older People in a Variety of Settings

By now it is apparent that there is great diversity among the elderly. Given the differences among older people, it is impossible to discuss their needs as if they were a homogeneous group or to develop a single program to meet all of their needs. One way to avoid these problems is to consider the separate needs of subgroups within the elderly population. We began to do this in Chapter 1 when we presented a chart showing the different needs of the well-elderly living in the community, of those with severe impairments, and of those in nursing homes. In this section, we will expand the discussion to more systematically consider the needs of the well-elderly in Chapter 5, of the homebound in Chapter 6, and of nursing home residents in Chapter 7. Additionally, in Chapter 8, we will consider the needs of older people as they approach their death.

Chapter Five

The Well-Elderly
in the Community

Contrary to the stereotype of being frail and feeble-minded, most persons over the age of sixty-five are in relatively good health and live on their own in the community. Roughly 80 percent of all those over sixty-five comprise the well-elderly. The newcomer to church, however, would find it difficult to identify all well-elderly congregants. The oldest of the old may stand out, but not the well-elderly. Many of the characteristics that once were indicative of being "old" are no longer applicable today. Roles are changing for both the young and old. Bernice Neugarten (1982) has written: "The society is becoming accustomed to the 70-year-old student, the 30-year-old college president, the 22-year-old mayor, and 35-year-old grandmother, the 50-year-old retiree, the 65-year-old father of a preschooler, and even the 85-year-old mother caring for her 65-year-old son" (p. 21).

Neugarten also reminds us that the group of people that she calls the young-old are not defined by their age, but by "health and social characteristics." They have not yet suffered from the major illnesses that plague the very old. Age is not the most significant factor shaping one's life. The accumulation of life experiences and current health status are far more important in determining quality of life. With good health comes greater potential for independence, freedom to do things, and the ability to fully be a part of the life and ministry of the church or synagogue.

Characteristic of the young-old years is time and energy for community participation. Now, for example, most people look forward to retirement and plan for the kinds of activities they wish to pursue afterward (see, for example, Atchley, 1976, and Robinson, Coberly, and Paul, 1985). Both retired persons and their spouses must adopt new roles and fill their time in meaningful ways. One way to do so is to provide for the needs of others through church and synagogue activities. Indeed, most people have a need to share with, help, and be of service to others. For Jewish people, this need reflects the value "tsedakah," giving to others as a form of social justice. How to facilitate these kinds of personally meaningful activities among the elderly is central to ministry with the well-elderly, as it is with all the elderly and, indeed, with persons of all ages.

Diminished opportunities for meaningful and constructive help to others occurs when people relocate from their life-long familiar environment or when their community changes. Most elderly, however remain in the same place in which they have reared their families; that is, the elderly "age-in-place." When the community has changed, although their familiar neighborhood and home may provide comfort, it is in many ways a different place with unfamiliar faces. In turn, a not uncommon occurrence is to move to a retirement community where new attachments to others, as well as to church and synagogue, must be developed. Some of these folks are "snowbirds" who maintain a summer residence in the north and a winter residence in the south.

Each living pattern presents a unique challenge to church and synagogue. Because, for example, elderly individuals who travel are clearly unavailable to be a part of the life and ministry of the congregation while they are away, it is difficult, at best, for them to hold leadership responsibilities in the congregation. The snowbirds present a particular problem for those Protestant denominations that do not allow their members to hold memberships in more than one church simultaneously. It is not uncommon, however, for an elderly person for whom church or synagogue is important, to hold full membership in two churches or synagogues, one in the south and one in the north. On the other hand, elderly who have aged-in-place present another kind of challenge. Although belonging to the church or synagogue that they joined many years ago, they feel alienated because of the changes in the life of the congregation. Fortunately, these instances also provide opportunities to congregations. People who have been members of a church or synagogue for many years can help interpret the traditions of the congregation to the next generation of members. Persons from other parts of the country bring in new ideas and new ways of doing things. Older people can always be an invaluable source of volunteer help and often contribute more financial resources than do younger members.

Needs of the Well-Elderly

Health is critical to being able to remain independent. All elderly must have access to proper medical services, particularly to preventive health care. One problem occurs when the elderly person outlives his or her doctor. Another kind of problem is the "ageism" of the medical profession. Field (1972) notes, "All too often, the physicians' responses to the complaints of the sick-elderly are: "You are getting on, you know? What can you expect? The machinery is wearing out.'" This attitude is much too frequent even today. Frequently, problems such as memory loss are passed off as "old age" and never adequately diagnosed.

The emotional needs of the elderly are also important. Some unmet emotional needs may have existed for many years, whereas others may begin in the later years. One obvious emotional need is for independence. Ironically, being independent necessitates being dependent on others. The more meaningful persons and social institutions an elderly person can depend on for support, the more independent he or she can be. Family and financial resources provide more options to enhance life. And, obviously, churches and synagogues can support independence needs of the elderly by providing a caring community, as well as concrete services.

Also needed is help in coping with loss. Some decline in health, the death of a spouse of friend, reduction in financial income, even a reduction in the ability to taste food are only some of the losses faced by the aging. Support of persons who are experiencing these and other losses involves helping the grief process. Unlike the loss of a close relative due to death, many of the losses of the elderly may seem to us to be of little significance. We must remember, however, that several "little" losses can add up to a big need to express feelings to someone who can empathize with them and help to place things in perspective. Beyond the clergy's personal response to congregants who are having an emotional crisis, the elderly themselves can act as peer counselors. Moreover, individual members of the congregation may have expertise and experiences that can be helpful to an elderly person, such as knowledge of pension benefits for the woman who has recently been widowed and does not realize to what she is entitled, or assistance in finding new living arrangements near others his age for the recently widowed man.

Social needs of older people can be difficult to meet, particularly since there are people who do not wish to belong to groups that are "for seniors." Fortunately, the name of the group is less important than its availability to serve the needs of the elderly. For example, in many churches and synagogues the women's clubs, men's clubs, fellowships or sisterhoods are de facto "senior clubs" because they are composed largely of older people. In addition to some seniors afraid to be stigmatized as old, there are others whose limited social skills make it difficult for them to join in clubs or church or synagogue activities. They do not know how to meet new people or how to "break the ice" when meeting someone for the first time. Some of these elderly have depended upon their spouses to lead them into social activities and to help them to feel comfortable among others. When these spouses die, they find it difficult to join in available activities. Still another group of elderly are those who have aged-in-place and who have previously had a large group of friends. Now they are older, those friends have moved away or even died and are no longer available. Without this group of old friends, the person is lonely. Although participation in a senior club would help reduce the loneliness, if they have not used the skills involved in making new friends for many years, it can be difficult to do so now.

Social programs for the elderly also need to include activities which go beyond social functions. Programs, for example, can maintain and promote health and wellness. Like persons of other ages, those becoming elderly are increasingly seeking activities that keep them healthy. Exercise programs and nutrition classes are important additions to the card clubs and travel lectures. Another kind of activity that is particularly relevant to the well-elderly is their wish to understand how they can maintain viable roles in community affairs. For example, many older persons want to know about programs which affect them, as well as discuss social and political issues. They are interested in the debates on Social Security and Medicare. Further, when they volunteer, the elderly wish to do things that are meaningful and to feel that they have made a contribution to the welfare of the community, church or synagogue, and other individuals.

The need for spiritual well-being was detailed in Chapter 2. Here, we will only focus on how faith may be one of the most persistent things for older people when other things are changing. Even the church or synagogue may change physically with new banners suspended from stately columns or rafters, new hymnals in the pews, and a new minister, priest, or rabbi. The God that will never change has done some mysterious housecleaning! When elderly complain about the changes, clergy often do not know how to respond. Yet change is inevitable, as the elderly certainly understand from their own lives. Clergy can assure, as well as demonstrate to elderly, that change and stability are not at all incompatible. The task is to support the elderly individual's ability to stay in touch with the old symbols and meaning that are still important, while maintaining contact with his or her religious community as it really is. Reaffirming the meaning of the old symbols, as a way of reaffirming the person for whom the symbols are meaningful, can indeed be made compatible with the growth needs of the congregaton. To do so necessitates working it out so that the strengths of both the old and the new are maximized.

Numerous needs have been mentioned in this chapter. Important needs of the well-elderly include physical needs encompassing access to health prevention information and services, to medical care when needed, to nonageist medical care, and to the necesary financial resources to pay for proper medical services. Psychological needs encompass maintaining independence, help with adjusting to loss, assistance with adjusting to new roles, and availability of caring persons for support. Social needs include opportunities to pursue personal interests, places where the elderly person feels comfortable meeting new people, a variety of fun and meaningful social activities, and a variety of meaningful volunteer opportunities. Meeting spiritual needs necessitates opportunities to reaffirm one's faith through participating in church or synagogue, opportunities to observe and share traditions which are part of one's faith, being with a caring group of people, and providing to the community and to others.

The Role of the Church and Synagogue

Churches and synagogues have been quietly providing services for the elderly in their congregations and communities for many years. Social service agencies, we have found, however, only have a vague idea of what religious groups do for the elderly and seldom know the extent of these efforts. Yet churches and synagogues do a great deal, as shown in Chart 5–1 which presents a summary of our surveys of four communities. The chart makes clear that churches and synagogues together are actually providing a wide range of services for seniors. Any single church or synagogue however, that attempts to provide the many services on the list would quickly realize the enormity of the task. Yet many religious organizations provide useful programs for not only their members but also for other persons from the local community. About half of the churches and synagogues, for example, have some kind of senior citizen's club or center. Approximately three-fourths reported the availability of transportation, at least to church or synagogue activities. Additionally, over three-quarters of these organizations provided counseling, as well as information and referral services. Clearly, the most common type of ministry is that of visitation to hospitals and the homebound.

Many of these services do not fall into the category of typical religious activities, such as worship services. These special services are provided for one of two reasons: either the program sponsored by the church or synagogue is not offered by any other group in the local community; or, while it exists in the local community, the church or synagogue would like to provide a program that reflects its own values or the needs of its own congregation. Thus, a club for the elderly may be developed simply because none exists in the local community or, on the other hand, because it can reflect the values or the needs of a specific congregation. No matter the motivation, it was clear in our surveys that these programs met some of the vital needs ofthe elderly in their communities.

Mainstreaming

A first consideration when developing programs for the well-elderly must be "mainstreaming." This simply means including the elderly in the diverse activities that already exist in the church or synagogue. To do so may necessitate removing physical barriers. Many churches and synagogues have flights of stairs that made attendance impossible for those who have difficulty in walking. Some places of worship have installed ramps and elevators while those with less money have asked ushers to stand out at the curb, rather than inside the building, to help members of the congregation up the stairs.

A problem that a church or synagogue may encounter in mainstreaming is the difficulties elderly have with hearing.

Chart 5–1
Programs Offered by Churches and Synagogues
in Four Communities*

	Percentage	
	Range	*Average*
1. Religious Programs		
Bible studies for seniors	0–76%	38%
Special worship for seniors	0–38%	25%
Holiday food baskets	53–71%	60%
2. Assistance to Participate in Church Activities		
Public address system	76–88%	82%
Assistance for people walking up stairs	62–76%	69%
Transportation to church or synagogue activities	63–100%	76%
Hearing aids for use during worship	10–22%	16%
Hearing aids in other parts of church/ synagogue	5–12%	8%
3. Leisure Activities		
Senior citizen clubs, groups, or circles	17–56%	38%
Meals where seniors gather at a central dining area	17–56%	38%
Education or discussion groups for seniors	0–47%	25%
Discussion groups on aging issues for younger people	10–41%	23%
4. General Support Programs		
Food distribution program	33–62%	45%
Free clothing	9–35%	24%

*Clergy were interviewed in four quite different communities regarding programs offered in their church or synagogue: 32 clergy in an ethnic working class community, 21 clergy in a racially mixed working class community, 6 clergy in a small more rural white-collar suburban community, and 34 clergy in a relatively affluent white-collar suburban community.

Chart 5–1 (continued)
Programs Offered by Churches and Synagogues
in Four Communities*

	Percentage	
	Range	*Average*
General transportation	0–62%	35%
Counseling for seniors	67–100%	85%
Counseling for families about aging or older relative	67–94%	78%
Information and referral	0–81%	38%
Intergenerational programs (i.e., adopt-a-grandparent)	10–33%	22%

5. Special Programs for the Hospitalized and Homebound

Visitation to the hospitalized and homebound	91–100%	96%
Visitation programming for people in nursing homes	88–91%	90%
Telephone reassurance	0–71%	38%
Home-delivered meals	6–33%	23%
Assistance with housekeeping	13–38%	25%

6. Training and Recognition of Lay Volunteers

Training for volunteers working with the elderly	5–29%	19%
Programs to recognize senior volunteers	0–17%	11%

Many churches or synagogues report that they do not have amplification systems available outside of the main worship area. Meeting rooms and other gathering points need to have some sort of amplification system available. Even when assistance is provided, however, such as hearing aids in the worship area, the elderly do not want to use the assistance. It is indeed difficult for many older people to admit that they have these kinds of special needs. Some elderly have a type of hearing loss that yields only minimal benefit from amplification. For this group, simply talking slowly or more distinctly is more effective than even the best of electronic equipment.

Another problem in mainstreaming is transportation. For some elderly, simply inviting them to ride alone with someone who lives nearby may yield a greater response than an advertisement that the church or synagogue bus is available. Too often the bus has high stairs making it difficult to climb. Obviously, these kinds of assistance must be tailored to individual elderly persons in the congregation.

Another kind of barrier is the increasing number of night programs. Many religious groups do most of their programming at night to meet the need of younger families and working couples. Unfortunately, however, many elderly are afraid to go out in the evening, and, as a result, they simply cannot be a part of the portion of the life of the church or synagogue.

Another aspect of mainstreaming pertains to intergenerational relationships. Aging occurs in families, and it is expected that adult children are concerned about the current and future needs of their aging parents. They struggle with questions such as, what will happen if Mom gets sick, or what will we do if Dad no longer can take care of himself? These questions need to be adressed. Equally important to address are anxieties expressed in a statement such as, I hope I am not like *that* when I grow old! It is helpful to adult children to attend discussion groups or adult education classes where these feelings can be verbalized and dealt with.

Intergenerational programming must also be extended to nonfamilial groups. Indeed, the essence of mainstreaming is to enhance interaction across age groups in creating a community in which the elderly are welcomed and participate actively with persons of all ages and contribute to their welfare.

If a holistic approach is truly to be achieved, then mainstreaming must include an appreciation for the uniqueness of the elderly. To be an integral part of the religious congregation, they must be incorporated into all its activities and know that they are making a contribution to the life of the church or synagogue. This must be done with a sensitivity to how the elderly achieve a sense of wholeness and inner peace: that is, how the elderly weave the strands of their life into an understanding of themselves with which they can be comfortable and in which they have a sense of spiritual well-being.

Programs Specifically for the Well-Elderly

Although mainstreaming should be an important emphasis for the well-elderly, special programs should also be developed just for seniors. Because the elderly have more available time, special religious programs can be developed with and for them. For example, a Bible study would be an appropriate group in most congregations, with the elderly providing direction and leadership. Yet, it should be understood that the charcteristics of the study group may have to be somewhat different than those for younger people. For instance, older people, more than younger ones, want to share their experiences and time needs to be allowed for them to do so.

Recreational and other kinds of socialization opportunities are essential, and it is the church or synagogue that often has available space. The federally funded nutrition programs have encouraged the development of congregate dining programs in churches and synagogues. Other activities, such as senior clubs, can be excellent programs for the elderly. In some churches and synagogues these clubs can benefit from the fact that these organizations also have programs, and even schools, for children. Many churches, synagogues and community agencies have found that programs that combine the generations are of benefit to both.

children
+
elders

The well-elderly are not a homogeneous group. Some, indeed, may be having problems in everyday living. Peer counseling programs should be considered. Programs specific to widows have also been successful. Widow-to-widow groups are appropriate in churches and synagogues. This kind of program suggests the questions, when should programs be developed just for the elderly, and when would the elderly be included in programs for all ages? Although there are no universal rules, two questions can guide decisions: what do we expect participants to gain from the program, and what approach do prospective participants prefer? If a program is to be provided that would be of interest to everyone, and if we can provide it at a time when everyone can participate, mainstreaming is appropriate. On the other hand, some programs like senior clubs are best directed at the elderly because they address some of the special needs of this age group. Often, if there are too few elderly to justify the expense of offering such a program, it could either be shared with the elderly from another church or synagogue, or it could be opened up to everyone in the congregation. In all these efforts, as indeed in all initiatives, the elderly must be able to give of themselves through church or synagogue and community. Work must be with the elderly, and their contributions valued.

Chapter Six

Enabling the Homebound

One of the oldest ways that churches and synagogues have addressed the needs of the elderly is through their ministries to the sick and shut-in. Mandated both by biblical and institutional traditions home visitation has taken place for thousands of years and continues in the vast majority of religious congregations today. Visitation remains the cornerstone of ministries to the homebound. Although it is the rare church or synagogue that does not have a ministry to the homebound, the pastoral literature contains numerous testimonies of dissatisfaction with current visitation approaches. One author (Vowler, 1983) begins with the question, Why don't pastors visit anymore? The pastor to whom this question was addressed does visit, yet studies of visitation have suggested that this may not be enough (see, for example, Malcolmson, 1980).

In this chapter, we shall examine both the needs of the shut-in elderly and ministries to them. When discussing ministerial approaches to the homebound, we shall move beyond pastoral visitation to the utilization of lay visitors, especially older adults, and linkages with local social service agencies.

Who are the Homebound Elderly?

We have suggested in earlier chapters that most older people are not homebound. Our best estimate is that, at any one time, about 8 percent of those over sixty-five are homebound, with over one-fourth of the group being bedridden (Shanas, et al., 1968). Indeed, there are more homebound elderly than there are elderly living in institutional settings. Overall, for every nursing home resident, there are at least two elderly living in the community requiring similar kinds of care.

When churches or synagogues reflect on the kinds of elderly in their congregations, a simple distinction is often made between the well-elderly who are still active in church or synagogue and the shut-ins who are not able to participate in the life of the church or synagogue. Elderly shut-ins, however, are not all alike. We have identified four rather distinct groups: (1) the temporarily homebound elderly, (2) the service shut-ins, (3) the chronically sick and bedfast elderly living in community settings, and, finally, (4) the caretakers of the elderly (Ellor and Tobin, 1985).

1. THE TEMPORARILY HOMEBOUND: These elderly have had a recent acute illness, such as a hip fracture or an infectious disease, and are now in the recovery phase. The temporarily homebound, like other elderly, have chronic diseases that slow or complicate recovery. Chronic illnesses reflect long-term disease processes that are not fully cured, such as arthritis. Eighty-five percent of people age sixty-five and over have one or more of these chronic diseases. Most older people, however, cope adequately with these infirmities and do not become temporarily or permanently homebound. In contrast, an acute condition is a temporary condition that generally can be treated. This can be a flare-up of a chronic condition. With time, the individual generally returns to his prior state of health and is no longer homebound.

2. THE SERVICE SHUT-IN: This second group of home-bound elderly is not generally recognized by churches or synagogues or social service agencies. These elderly have become isolated and homebound because they do not have access to the services that would enable them to remain active in the community. They are often difficult to identify because, when they occasionally attend church or synagogue, they appear to be quite well, and, when asked, they usually tell their clergy that everything is fine. Upon investigation, however, they may be quite lonely and feel as though they are becoming detached from church, synagogue and community. Some are homebound simply because they are unable to drive or drive only when the weather is good. Others may be seasonally homebound, becoming isolated in the winter and other times of the year when the weather is poor. Finally, some may be unable to leave their home for emotional reasons. Unresolved grief after losing a spouse may, for example, cause a physically healthy senior to be home-bound. Generally, if services such as transportation or counseling are provided, they would be able to return to active participation in congregational and community life. When these services are not available, however, our observations suggest that they are likely to become quite bitter and withdrawn. Ironically, since they have not been recognized as homebound, they have not been visited or included in other ministries for the homebound.

3. THE CHRONICALLY SICK AND BEDBOUND: The third group are the chronically ill shut-ins who usually live with a spouse or with their children but occasionally live alone. Typically, they have multiple physical and emotional limitations and tend to be on the permanent shut-in calling lists of churches or synagogues. They also may be on the lists of local social service and home-health care agencies. Thus, ministry with this group of elderly may be enhanced by conversations and coordination with visiting nurses and other home-health care personnel.

4. THE CARETAKERS OF THE ELDERLY: Caretakers may also be homebound due to their responsibilities in the home. Caretakers are frequently elderly wives of impaired husbands or children in their sixties who may not be able to get out of the house because there is no one else to care for their sick loved one. These caretakers have a different set of needs than the bedfast or confused older person for whom they provide care and supervision. Their needs, however, are often overlooked when attention is focused upon their relative, who is more readily identified as someone in need of help.

The Needs of Shut-in Seniors

To determine the needs of a homebound elderly, we must begin by identifying to which of the four groups he or she belongs. The elderly person recovering from an acute illness is likely to be very interested in getting well and returning to previous activities, while the elderly person who is chronically ill needs to work toward adjusting to his or her impairments. In turn, service shut-ins need help to get out before becoming too sick to ever leave their homes again. Finally, too many caretakers do not recognize a need to be concerned about themselves and are preoccupied with the needs of the sick family member. Regardless of the type of shut-in, the visitor must listen and respond to the senior, based on his or her unique needs.

Since it is not possible to identify universal needs for shut-ins, two vignettes wil be used here to illustrate some of the feelings that must be considered when working with homebound seniors and their family caretakers.

Mrs. Alexander is a 61-year-old divorced woman who has multiple sclerosis and lives alone. She has no family nearby and lives in subsidized housing on a limited income. The church is very important to her. She attends a church other than her own because her church does not provide transportation to services. She would prefer to attend her own church, but there is no one who is willing to pick her up and assist her up the stairs. She does not want to blame the church, as she understands that "they are probably very busy." However, she is particularly annoyed at the lay people and considers it terrible that none visits. "No one has called except the pastor. . . .I don't know many people, but I did belong to the prayer group, and they know I'm sick." She feels she could be more active if she could have some assistance with stairs and transportation. However, particularly in the winter, she often is unable to go out for months at a time.

Mrs. Goldstein is a 76-year-old woman who has recently moved from New York City to Florida with her husband. Prior to the move, she had been the president of the sisterhood at their synagogue and an important person in the congregation. In Florida, she has been dissatisfied with the rabbi because he does not treat her with the same respect as the one "back home." She had only just begun to get to know people when she fell and broke her hip. Now she is unable to leave her home, and her husband is afraid to leave her alone for long periods of time. Thus he, too, has curtailed his activities. Both feel abandoned by the synagogue and the rabbi because they have been neither visited nor even phoned to see how they are doing.

As is apparent in these vignettes, loneliness and fear of continued illness are typical concerns. Although not unique to the elderly who are homebound, these feelings become more intense when the individual is shut-in. For them, a schedule of home visits should be developed that extends over weeks and even months. Most critical is the need for congregations to examine their current ministry to shut-ins and determine whether or not they have found ways of hearing the variety of needs expressed by the elderly and assessing what they can do about them.

Major Concerns in Working with the Homebound

The task of supporting the spiritual well-being of the homebound elderly must begin by getting to know the whole person. Because we interact differently with others depending on the setting, a visitor who knows the person at church or synagogue may discover a quite different person at home, particularly if an illness has occurred. Getting to know the whole person requires the visitor to be able to move beyond the small talk of everyday conversation and to be open to the physical, social, psychological, and spiritual sides of the person. Even more important than gaining a sensitivity to the several facets of a person is to begin to understand how the parts fit together and comprise a whole person. It is not sufficient to interpret a statement like "I feel so useless" as simply a lack of activities. Rather, it is necessary to understand how the older person feels about losses of physical abilities, of people with whom to interact, and of self-esteem. Not uncommon, when the visitor is open to the person, are revealing queries like why has my family abandoned me, or why won't God let me die? Some of these concerns for spiritual well-being that affect the homebound elderly, their families, and the community will be examined in the next section.

Concerns of the Elderly

Unlike the very old person who moves into a nursing home, the homebound older person does not experience a change in living situation along with the changes in his health status. Rather, homebound elderly probably have lived in their current locations for most of their lives and retain this attachment. Strong bonds that have been created with the place lived in for a long time are reflected in memories, both good and bad, of events and people that are associated with it. For many elderly, however, the people they have known are no longer available to them. Friends may have died or moved away, and those still in the community may be too sick themselves to visit. Alternately, they may have many visitors immediately after returning from the hospital but very few thereafter. Concern for the spiritual well-being of the elderly must be directed toward helping to retain continuity in their life, in spite of their many losses. Personal faith provides needed continuity and may be one of the few supports available to them for comfort and reassurance. An illustration:

> Mrs. Jensen is a 79-year-old widow who lives alone. Although she is still active, she is afraid of falling. Her church is very important to her: "it's my heavenly home on earth. I feel terrible when I can't go." Her son takes her to church on Sundays, but if he is not available she watches religious services on television. Twenty years ago she was president of the Women's Society. She would like to be more active now, but she cannot because of her bad arthritis. She has difficulty finding people to talk to on the telephone because so many of her friends have died, moved out of the area to live with family, or are unable to hear well enough to carry on a conversation. She feels that her greatest problem is loneliness.

The homebound, such as Mrs. Jensen, also need physical care, often complete bed care. Further fears related to future needs may be as painful as current needs. A common fear, for example, is falling while getting up at night to use the bathroom. An additional concern of the homebound comes from the necessity to adapt homes to disabilities, such as placing grab bars by the shower and in other locations in the bathroom, removing throw rugs to avoid stumbling over them, and modifying sleeping arrangements, as occurs when placing the bed from the upstairs bedroom in the living room because steps to the second floor cannot be negotiated. These changes can be quite disorienting. Ministries to the homebound can help the elderly by assisting in providing care, adapting their homes, and making adjustments to the changes in their environments.

Concerns with the Families

The spiritual well-being of family members can neither be separated from the relationship with the impaired relative, nor from their concerns about providing care for him. When visitors begin to become acquainted with a homebound elderly person they will generally hear something about that person's family. Independent of whether the relationship portrayed is positive or negative, it reflects a relationship that has developed and persisted over many years. Although many families are capable of modifying their relationships, old patterns still exist in some form. Family patterns, such as sibling rivalry, the favorite child, the family scapegoat or the family rescuer, are reflected in such comments as, Jane is always there when I need her (implying that the other children are not), or Bill is the oldest so he handles my affairs. Along with these old patterns come old feelings, both good and bad, that will effect the way family members currently relate to each other and their aging parent and reflect both emotional and spiritual well-being.

Families as caretakers are obviously of importance to the homebound senior. They supply 70 to 80 percent of all the social service needs of the elderly (see, for exmaple, Comptroller General of the United States, 1977). When family members become caretakers, they provide for many needs of their impaired relative. They must give physical assistance in caring for the elderly person, as well as emotional support. In turn, family members need help from others in providing physical and emotional support to their homebound family member. And they may need help to feel it is all right to go out and to enjoy themselves. At the very least, they must be able to go out shopping, run errands, and have short vacations. An example is the following:

> Mr. and Mrs. Erdman are both over ninety years old. Mrs. Erdman has a number of chronic illnesses but was still able to get out of the house until her husband became ill. About two years ago Mr. Erdman suddenly had a stroke while working in the yard. After a brief period in the hospital, he returned home but has not been able to walk

since then. Mrs. Erdman does everything for him. She makes his meals, helps him go to the bathroom and talks with him to keep his mind active. She would like to get out of the house to go to church and return to her senior center activities but feels that she can not leave her husband alone. Since there is no one else to stay with him, she remains at home.

Although the Erdman's did not do so, family members often turn to their clergy for help with questions such as, should we continue to care for father at home or put him in a nursing home, and how much should we do for mother or how much should we allow her to do for herself? Two rules of thumb may be useful. First, as much as possible, impaired elderly persons should be allowed to make their own decisions. Making decisions about the future is essential to feeling independent. The second rule is that when physical caregiving becomes so taxing on the family that members have neither the time nor the energy simply to be themselves, it is necessary to obtain outside help. Some caretakers feel guilty seeing outside help because they feel they are shirking responsibilities. They must be assured that it is appropriate to do so and that the assistance will make it easier for them to provide their emotional support, which cannot be bought at any price. Also when the burden of providing care becomes overwhelming, they may have to be assured that nursing home care is appropriate.

Concerns in Maintenance of Community Support

Community support for homebound elderly is of vital importance, yet is not always available. Elderly who are homebound may have dropped out of community activities very slowly. Their friends may have moved, died, or become equally shut-in. The clergy and other key community leaders may have moved to other locations and been replaced by new people whom they do not know. In short, it is easy for an elderly person who is homebound to become cut off and feel isolated, alone in an ever-shrinking world. Thus, the maintenance of ties to the community can be a vital link to the current realities of the church or synagogue and community. Whether visitors come to talk or also to provide some sort of needed service, they are important to the general well-being of any shut-in. Visitors provide stimulation and let the person know they are still part of the community. An illustration follows:

> Miss Peters, who never married, is eighty-two years old and lives alone in an apartment. Concerned about enough things to keep busy, she reads a great deal and watches television. However, she wishes she could find more people with whom to talk. She has been confined to a wheelchair following an unsuccessful knee operation in 1975, and now her greatest fear is that someone will find out she lives alone and will break into her home. She has been a member of a church for over fifty years, but it is in a changing neighborhood. Also, she has not been able to keep in touch since the last pastor left. She knows that the new minister must be busy with all of the local community problems but wonders if there is not someone left from the old congregation who would be willing to visit here. She observes her religious faith by reading religious magazines and especially enjoys reading the Bible. Private prayers are also important to her, and she listens to religious programs on television and radio.

Concern for the spiritual well-being of the homebound older persons requires more than discussing a Bible verse or talking about the church or synagogue or having a prayer. Required is an awareness of the needs of the whole person and his or her family and a genuine interest in the health and emotional well-being of the shut-in which enhances his or her faith and spiritual well-being.

Current Programs for the Homebound

Since about 1965 numerous services have become available to assist the homebound elderly. While a few agen-

cies like the Visiting Nurse Association and the Red Cross
have been available for much longer, the availability of
money from the government has dramatically increased the
number of services in most communities. Although services
for the homebound vary from state to state and community
to community, in most areas several types of services exist.
Present in most communities will be a visiting nurse program, Meals-on-Wheels, hospital equipment supply stores,
and transportation programs for persons in wheelchairs.
Other services like telephone reassurance, friendly visitors,
and in-home counseling services may also be available.
Churches and synagogues must investigate the various types
of programs for the homebound elderly that exist in the local
community by asking: "What programs currently exist?"
and if the programs exist: "Are they adequate to meet the
need?" Particularly in a climate of programmatic cutbacks,
many agencies have continued to provide the service, but
have lengthy waiting lists for service. These waiting lists may
be so long that by the time an individual elderly person's request for service gains a response, he or she no longer has
the need. Where this situation exists, the church or
synagogue may choose to support the expansion of an existing service rather than create a new one.

Whether the church or synagogue is aiding a program
that is currently unable to meet all of the vast needs in its area
or developing a new one, most of the services listed above
can be delivered by churches and synagogues. For example,
by supplying elderly volunteer drivers to a Meals-on-Wheels
program, more meals can be delivered. A group of retired
persons in the church or synagogue who have cars can help
out when transportation is needed to drive seniors to see
their physicians. In turn, programs developed by the elderly,
like telephone reassurance and friendly visiting, may already
exist in the church or synagogue but need to be coordinated
with other groups. For example, one church that was sending someone to visit a local man in a retirement hotel found that
a nearby Bible college was also sending people to visit him.
The Bible college student came on Tuesday morning, and the
church representative visited him Tuesday evening. Thus,
the man had two groups that visited him, yet he was alone

for six days of the week. Another example is the ladies club that telephones shut-ins to see how they are doing. If they were made aware of other elderly who were not members of the church but who would appreciate a call, they could expand their ministry of calling to others. It is important for any church or synagogue to be in contact with local service agencies for the homebound in an effort to at least communicate with them about what they are doing and, it is hoped, to coordinate expand their efforts.

The Role of Church and Synagogue
in Serving the Homebound

The role of church and synagogue in working with the homebound elderly reflects their versatility. Other social service agencies and professions are restricted in their work with the homebound by guidelines which limit whom they can visit and narrowly define both the purpose and duration of the visit. The church or synagogue visitor (along with some publicly-funded "friendly visitor programs'") have greater flexibility to meet whatever needs are perceived. Thus, persons can be visited who may not be too sick or may be simply in need of transportation rather than concrete medical or social services. If a loaf of bread is needed, the church or synagogue visitor does not have to check the local public aid guidelines or fill out an intake form. This visitor thus is able to provide "services" that may be difficult, if not impossible, for other types of social service agencies to provide.

Above all, church and synagogue visitors are not working alone because they are connected philosophically and programmatically to a group of caring people. When visitors do not know the elderly person, they still represent the congregation and can help in maintaining contact with religious feelings and religious institutions. There is a universality to church and synagogue that can be used symbolically to support the meaning of the elderly person's faith. The visitor brings some portion of the religious institution as it is today.

Churches and synagogues, with all of their problems and changes, are still communities of people of all ages, even older adults, that care enough to visit.

Current Models of Homebound Ministry

Examination of our data suggests four general models of shut-in ministry that can be found. The first is the clergy-focused ministry. Although there may be some lay visitation, clergy are often only vaguely aware of it, and thus no effort is made to coordinate visitation. This often occurs where there is only one ordained clergy. While they seem to know their congregants, and indicate that they know when a visit is appreciated, they have little or no organized schedule or list of seniors for their visitation. They do not seem to consider doing any sort of systematic survey of the needs of the elderly and appear to be very comfortable with their approach.

The second model is that of shared clergy-laity visitation. Clergy who utilize this model note that alone with those persons whom they visit, they are aware of and encourage visitation by lay persons in the congregaton. Members from groups such as the board of deacons, or the women's fellowship, or the sisterhood are frequently mentioned as engaged in visitation. Yet the role of the group is often unclear. Although this model involves more persons in the visitation process, there remains little interest in organizing their combined efforts. A comprehensive list of either visitors or visitees is generally unavailable, and no effort is made to coordinate visits by either clergy or laity. Nor are efforts made to incorporate the older congregants into the visitation program, thereby missing an especially effective resource. When a system is lacking, it is assumed that visitors simply know when they are needed and visit when they can. Usually, only when a problem arises are the clergy, the church or synagogue board, or fellowship notified.

The third model, found most frequently in the larger multiple staff churches, employs the use of a minister of visitation, where a single person is hired for this purpose.

When this ministry is narrowly defined as exclusively for the shut-ins of the congregation, the person is usually found to be either a retired Protestant minister or a Catholic nun. Other clergy and laity in these churches may do some visitation, but the central figure is the minister of visitation (or pastoral care). These individuals generally work from specific calling lists but may, or may not, coordinate their efforts with other clergy, lay boards, or other church members. When reference is made to a ministry to the elderly in these congregations, it is to this somewhat narrow activity.

The final model of systematic ministry is somewhat more complex and more organized than the first three. This model combines active clergy and lay involvement. It can be found in both large (over 500 members) and small (under 150 members) churches and synagogues which have higher percentages of homebound elderly. Some effort is made to establish the need for the ministry, as well as the individual needs of potential recipients, through congregational meetings, through visitation and through chats with visitors about the needs of individual homebound elderly. In some cases, it is through the use of a survey instrument. Whatever the approach, input is actively sought as to the needs for, and designs of, this ministry. This type of ministry is especially implemented by a specific group of clergy and visitors who have periodic meetings to train, enable, and support visitors. A concise coordinated list of visitees is used, though criteria for inclusion on the list may not be strictly defined. Finally, these ministries provide other services beyond visitation, such as either formally or informally organized transportation to church or synagogue, doctors' appointments, meals, support groups for caretakers, and other supportive services. While these groups generally struggle to have enough visitors and enough volunteers to provide services, they do attempt to provide a comprehensive range of services for the homebound or shut-in senior, and they do include the elderly in developing the system of homebound visitation.

Each of these models is perceived by clergy as meeting congregational need. Sometimes this is an appropriate perception, as when a suburban church with only a handful of elderly members uses the first model. If, however, the congregation is composed of 25 to 50 percent elderly and has a total membership of over a thousand, the first three models may not be adequate. The amount of organization and number of participants should correspond to need, not to some type of textbook mode.

Current Church and Synagogue Programs for the Homebound

Because at the heart of church and synagogue programs for the homebound is generally some type of visitation program, we included questions about ministries to the homebound in one of our community studies. Of the thirty-four churches in this community that responded to our survey, thirty-two (94 percent) have some type of ministry to the homebound, and thirty (89 percent) have some type of involvement from the lay persons of that church. (This figure may suggest a higher involvement of lay persons than is true in other areas because there was an active training program for visitors in the community sponsored by Catholic Charities.) Lay involvement varied from the unorganized contribution of an occasional individual who stops to see another parishioner to highly organized and trained programs of lay visitors. No matter how much lay involvement a church had, all churches had some involvement by clergy.

As we look at the various ministries, we note that selection of who should be visited was generally done by clergy. Often visits were initiated in response to requests from relatives, friends, and other members of the congregation. Many clergy noted that they responded to all requests, as well as to their own observations of need. The question of who should be visited is significant, because it is generally the point of entry into a visitation program or inclusion on the church's shut-in calling list. Although it may be hard for the church visitors to see everyone who would like a visit, unless the need for a contact is identified, the homebound individual may not be visited at all. One pastor noted, "My greatest frustration in the ministry is from the person who spends a week in the hospital, never tells anyone that they are there but, upon returning home, complains to all of their friends that 'no one at the church cares. They didn't even visit me when I was in the hospital' " The pastor went on to note, "I'm a priest, not a psychic!'

Many clergy struggle with decisions about how much time they should spend visiting. We found that no matter how many clergy are employed by the church or how many elderly are on the calling list, the large Catholic parishes (2,000 to 10,000 members) and the large protestant churches (400 to 1,500) average eleven hours of visitation per week, while the small Protestant churches (50 to 400 members) averaged five hours per week. These numbers differ from one parish and pastor to another, depending upon the amount of time needed on such tasks as administration, religious education, worship and other ministry and pastoral endeavors.

The purpose of the ministry to shut-ins is perceived somewhat differently by clergy and elderly. Most clergy noted that a major purpose of visitation is to show concern for the person (86 percent), while only 21.5 percent agreed that a major purpose is to meet religious/spiritual concerns. The responses of a small purposive sample of elderly (eighty three persons) was different. Almost one-half (46 percent) agreed that a major purpose was to provide a religious experience. Additionally, 45 percent also responded that a major purpose is to keep in touch with the church. And a lesser percentage of the elderly (40 percent) than the clergy felt that a major purpose is to show concern for the person. Thus while 86 percent of clergy perceived that a major purpose is to show concern, the elderly themselves are less likely to perceive this as a major purpose. In turn, the elderly are more likely than clergy to perceive the visit as important in providing a religious experience and in maintaining a physical tie with the church.

Finally, we asked about the content of the pastoral visits. Half of the clergy noted that they prefer to take a nondirectional approach when visiting shut-ins, allowing them to talk about whatever they wish. Three of four clergy mentioned things that they either liked or disliked about visits. Critical to their responses was the meaning of the visit. When clergy felt that they had a meaningful interaction with the older person, they felt good about the visit, but when the visit did not seem to be meaningful, then they did not have these positive feelings. Also, several clergy commented that they often felt that they learned more from the older person than the older person learned from them.

Conspicuous by its absence in these discussions with clergy are the goals for treatment or plans for care that are used by counseling and medical professionals. Other professionals evaluate the success or failure of their visits by whether or not they met some or all of their goals for the visit. Success for the clergy who do not set goals, however, can only be measured in terms of satisfaction and perceived appreciation. Paradoxically, it may well be the elderly individual who is uanble to express appreciation who most needs such a visit.

In essence, then, the church or synagogue visitor is probably someone who does not have the constraints found among social service agency personnel. This may allow them to be more flexible as to who is visited and what other tasks or services are provided. It may also make it more difficult to understand the significance of the visit, particularly if the older person is unable to express his or her feelings.

New Directions in Programming for the Homebound

While the actual visit is at the heart of the visitation ministry, many ministries have found that other activities can be of enormous importance to the well-being of the elderly. Although the religious organization may not be in a position to respond to all of the needs of the elderly, it is often evident that needs extend beyond the occasional visit. Unfortunately, homebound elderly generally have a great many unmet needs which churches and synagogues can not address because of too few volunteers, a lack of expertise and a paucity of resources.

Programs, such as Meals-on-Wheels, transportation assistance, shopping assistance, home maintenance and repair, telephone reassurance, and assistance with house-keeping tasks, can mean the difference between staying at home and having to move to a nursing home. Churches or synagogues that are unable to actually provide supportive services should at least become familiar with the services that are available in the community in order to utilize them or to be able to make a referral.

Program development for the needs of elderly persons' physical, psychological, social, and spiritual concerns are shown on Chart 6–1. Each program may necessitate a set of activities and many may require greater programming than a single church or synagogue can provide. Thus, programs should be developed selectively and often in collaboration with other churches and synagogues and with social service agencies. To facilitate the development of collaboration, the Robert Wood Johnson Foundation has funded interfaith coalitions to provide volunteer services to the homebound. Monsignor Charles Fahey is the director of this innovative program that will indeed enhance the lives of the elderly.

Maintaining A Holistic Orientation

Critical to the development of holistic programming is remembering that homebound elderly are persons who remain capable of ministry themselves. Too often the assumption is that the homebound person is no longer capable of contributing to the life of the congregation. Yet some churches and synagogues have found that impaired seniors can contribute in meaningful ways, even if the contributions are small. For example, a wheelchairbound person can use the telephone to make calls in a cheer ministry for the church or synagogue. Others may be able to collate, staple and fold church newsletters and bulletins and be involved in prayer ministry and Bible study. Creative use of the talents of this group can be helpful not only to the congregation but also to the psychological and spiritual well-being of the impaired elderly person.

Also important is that, although church and synagogue may not be able to provide for all of the elderlys' needs, they should be sufficiently sensitive to them so that they are able to make referrals to the appropriate professional or agency. Thus, if the person needs a doctor, clergy should not feel that they must provide medical services in order to support the whole person, but certainly referral to a physician is appropriate.

Program Ideas

Numerous program ideas have been developed for the homebound elderly. One way to learn about some of them is to find out what other churches and synagogues are doing. Some of the programs which we are aware of follow. Visitation programs are not listed, since most churches and synagogues already have some sort of regular visitation to the homebound.

Support programs for homebound elderly can include telephone reassurance programs and a cheer ministry sending letters or cards. Other ways to bring the life of the congregation to a homebound individual's residence including taping services, delivering worship bulletins and newsletters, making a special banner, gifts, flowers, photographs of friends from church, and so forth; developing Bible study programs in the homes of the homebound; a prayer ministry among the homebound, including them in prayer for others; indepth counseling and emotional support programs to address both spiritual and psychological issues; programs to exchange skills between youth and homebound seniors; service projects which can be done by homebound seniors for the congregation or other community groups; in-home assistance with tasks such as cooking, cleaning, shopping, running errands, and so forth; bringing special hot meals to the home; a transportation program which takes homebound elderly to church, doctors appointments, and other activities in the community; a home maintenance and repair program; assistance in making necessary structural changes in the

Chart 6–1
The Homebound Elderly
Needs and Programmatic Responses

Needs of Homebound Elderly	*Programmatic Responses*
Physical Needs	
. . . assistance with household tasks	――― develop a program with youth or adults who can help with cooking, cleaning, laundry, shopping, running errands, and so forth
. . . hot meals	――― assign dates and have someone bring in meals
. . . assistance with home maintenance and yard work	――― develop home maintenance and repair programs
. . . maintenance of personal hygiene	――― train specific individuals individuals to assist with bathing and personal care
. . . assistance in seeking medical care	――― train lay visitors on referral practice and provide transportation to medical appointments
. . . maintenance of a crime free environment	――― advocate with government for crime prevention; initiate a neighborhood watch program
Psychological Needs	
. . . maintenance of independence	――― develop programs that support physical needs and independent decisionmaking by the homebound
. . . support in coping with loneliness	――― regular visitation by groups from church
	――― transportation programs, help seniors to get out of the house
	――― telephone reassurance

Chart 6–1 (continued)

. . . assistance in dealing with loss --- pastoral counseling around grief issues

Social Needs

. . . maintenance of contact with church and community --- visitation ministry, telephone reassurance, letters, cards, and so forth

. . . feel like part of the church --- programs for transportation and senior involvement

. . . opportunities for service --- develop service projects which can be done in the home

. . . opportunities for meaningful social activities --- develop activities that can be shared by the homebound

Spiritual Needs

. . . opportunities to be a part of worship --- develop transportation and/or cassette ministries

. . . opportunities to minister to others --- provide opportunities to contribute to the ministry of the church

. . . opportunities to reflect on issues of faith --- visitation ministry

Needs of the Caregivers

. . . opportunities to leave home to do things on their own

Programmatic Responses

--- develop a group of persons who would be willing to spend brief periods of time with homebound seniors

. . . opportunities to do things themselves without feeling guilt and to have someone say thank you for helping, even if their sick relative is unable to do so --- develop a support group for caretakers

home to accommodate the needs of handicapped individuals; assistance in making or purchasing the equipment and adaptive devices which are needed by homebound individuals with handicaps; providing other financial and legal assistance as it is needed; and offering a program which coordinates services provided in the community (e.g., home-health care agencies and Meals-on-Wheels) and supplementing these activies with church and synagogue sponsored in-home services.

Support programs for caregivers were also needed, including developing a list of persons who would be willing to stay with the homebound elderly person for brief periods of time in order for the caretaker to be able to go out of the home.

Finally, support programs for visitors from churches or synagogues are essential, including training programs for visitors, development of teams of lay visitors, and support groups for visitation groups.

Very meaningful programs can be developed for the homebound, some by the church or synagogue alone, others in collaboration with other religious, as well as nonreligious, institutions.

Chapter Seven

Outreach to Nursing Home Residents

T he label "nursing homes" elicits powerful images for most people. Although often scorned, these facilities serve as home to over one million older Americans. Further, the number of elderly living in nursing homes is growing rapidly. Since 1960 the percentage of older people in nursing homes has doubled, increasing from 2.3 to 5.5 percent of those over sixty-five. It has been estimated by Vincente, Wiley and Carrington (1979) that as many as one in three older people will spend some period of time during their lives living in a nursing home.

About Nursing Homes

There are now about 20,000 institutions in the United States providing care to chronically ill people (see, for this statistic, as well as other statistics noted in this chapter, U.S. General Accounting Office, 1979, page 7; U.S. National Center for Health Statistics, 1979; U.S. National Center for Health Statistics, 1980, page 93; and U.S. Senate, Special Committee on Aging, 1981, pages 357-358). These institutions are called by a variety of names, such as nursing homes, long-term care facilities, convalescent centers, homes for the aged, rehabilitation centers, and health-care facilities. All exist to provide a range of services for older people who cannot live independently. Services provided by nursing homes can include medical and personal care, residential services, a therapeutic or rehabilitation program, and protective or custodial care.

It is difficult to make generalizations about all nursing homes, since there are so many different types of facilities. For example, nearly 80 percent of all nursing homes in the United States are run as profit-making businesses, while about 20 percent are operated by voluntary, nonprofit organizations, such as churches and synagogues and the government. Further, different nursing homes will provide different levels of care for residents. Skilled care facilities provide twenty-four hour care supervised by professionals, such as registered nurses, physical therapists, occupational therapists, and so forth. Intermediate care facilities also provide twenty-four-hour health care and supportive services, but these services are not as extensive as within a skilled care facility. Sheltered care or health-related facilities, which may include retirement homes, are designed for people who do not require extensive physical care but need room and board, as well as opportunities for socialization. A variety of other factors, including differences in state and local regulations and availability of funds, can affect the staffing, types of services, and the quality of care in the individual home.

Nursing Home Residents

The typical nursing home resident is a person of advanced old age with extensive health problems. The average age of nursing home residents is now nearly eighty-five and in many nursing homes more than one in four residents may be ninety or over. Most people enter a nursing home because of poor physical health. A variety of chronic illnesses are very common among residents, including hardening of the arteries, heart trouble, hypertension, and strokes. Over one-half may have chronic brain syndrome or mental illness. Regardless of whether their impairments are physical or psychological in nature, almost all nursing home residents need at least some assistance with personal care, such as bathing, dressing, toileting, walking, and eating. About 25 percent need assistance with all these activities, and only 10 percent of nursing home residents can perform these tasks independently. The remaining 65 percent of all residents need assistance with some combination of the tasks of daily living.

Even the occasional visitor to nursing homes will have observed that there are far more women than men living in these facilities. In fact, women outnumber men by a margin of nearly three to one. Unavailability of a spouse or family to care for the impaired older person influences nursing home placement and only 12 percent of all nursing home residents have a living spouse. Since loss of a spouse is more common for older women than older men, institutionlization is also more common for women. In addition, institutionalized older people are less likely to have family than their counterparts living in the community. Only about half of all nursing home residents have a living child, while four of five older people in the general population have at least one living child. This information clearly suggests that the existence of a health problem is not the sole reason an older person enters a nursing home. Most are without someone who can live with them or otherwise provide for their care, preventing the need for institutional care.

The Needs of Nursing Home Residents

In one sense, it is very artificial to discuss the needs of nursing home residents as if they were different from the needs of other people. The basic human needs of these people do not change when they enter a nursing home. They, as we, need a clean, safe, hospitable living environment; appropriate health care and nutrition; involvement with family, friends, and community; an opportunity to observe their faith; and a meaningful role in society. Just as do other people, nursing home residents need to be needed and to be involved in the world around them.

While the basic needs of institutionalized older people do not change, their circumstances are unique. As with other elderly, nursing home residents struggle to understand themselves in the face of multiple losses. For the nursing home resident, however, these losses are often of an extreme nature. For most, this includes decreasing physical and cognitive abilities. The body deteriorates and thought processes slow down. For some, losses also include the recent death of a spouse. Ties with family members and friends may also be shaken or severed when an older person enters a nursing home. This is particularly true for residents who move out of their neighborhoods to live closer to their children. When an older person has been active in church, synagogue, or community affairs, involvement generally decreases sharply or totally stops after entering a nursing home. In addition to these losses, many nursing home residents must give up their homes or apartments, often for financial reasons. This is very difficult for some because it not only means giving up an important part of their past lives but also diminishes their chances of ever leaving the nursing home. Further, because of the high cost of institutional care, many older people must spend all their savings before becoming eligible for government assistance to pay for their nursing home care.

These and many other types of losses are very common among nursing home residents. Any one loss is a great burden, but multiple losses can become totally overwhelming. Maintaining identity after losing those many things that have been an integral part of life is perhaps the most difficult task faced by a nursing home resident. A sense of depression and hopelessness is common. Hopelessness, according to Tobin (1966), can be understood as a "pervasive feeling that there is no future in one's life and that life has lost its meaning." (p.3).

Yet, adjusting to these losses is not the only psychological adjustment faced by nursing home residents. In addition, they must learn to accept new and very foreign living environments. Institutional life is strikingly different from life in a private residence. Schedules are set which regulate almost everything a resident might do. Not only do schedules control the activities which the resident can engage in, but they also dictate the amount of time a resident is allowed for any one task. Residents often feel that they have lost control of their lives when they are no longer allowed to make decisions about anything which is done to or for them. A sense of dependency and helplessness is very common among residents. These feelings become more intense when residents are treated more like children than mature adults.

Knowing that feelings of helplessnes and hopelessness are often at the root of residents' problems, it is possible to begin to better understand their needs. Three major needs then become apparent. First, a prominent need for residents is to participate in decisions about their lifestyle and care. To the greatest extent possible, residents should remain in control of these decisions. This includes making decisions about their health care, as well as when they will participate in recreational, social, and religious activities. Second, residents have a need to interact regularly with their family, friends, and community groups in which they have been active. Maintaining contact with their church or synagogue is often very important for residents. While they vary in the type and extent of contact desired, most nursing home residents want some sort of contact with groups outside the nursing home. Third, nursing home residents need a useful role in life. They must be free to pursue meaningful activities and interests, including finding ways to make significant contributions to others.

Obviously, residents will express these needs differently and want to act on them in a variety of ways. Further, because their physical, cognitive, and social skills range widely, not all residents are willing and able to participate in the same types of activities. Yet, it is important to realize that all residents, from the most impaired to the most well functioning, have these basic needs.

In addition to these psychological, social and spiritual needs, nursing home residents obviously have a great need for good physical care. As previously noted, many residents have a variety of physical illnesses and impairments, and because of their frail health status, most residents need regular medical attention. Most residents require assistance with personal care and hygiene, as well as careful attention to their nutritional needs. Good preventive health care is also important in helping residents maintain their highest level of functioning and avoiding preventable problems such as bed sores. Providing appropriate equipment, from eye glasses, hearing aides and dentures to devices to assist with walking, eating and dressing, is also very important but easily overlooked in some facilities. Attending to these physical needs not only adds to the comfort of residents but is essential in maintaining a high quality of life.

Physical, psychological, social, and spiritual needs, as shown in Chart 7-1, can indeed be extensive among nursing home residents.

Major Concerns in Working with Nursing Home Residents

Understanding the meaning of spiritual well-being in the nursing home is not an easy task. It is very difficult for many residents to find a way to say "yes to life" when they feel helpless, hopeless, and forgotten. Nursing homes are often viewed by residents, staff, and families as the end of the road—a place of death, not a place of life. Yet, helping residents find a way to live life to its fullest while living in the nursing home seems to be the essence of promoting and maintaining spiritual well-being in this setting. This means giving residents a chance to function as fully and independently as possible and develop their interests and abilities to their greatest potential.

A wide variety of factors work against the spiritual well-being of nursing home residents. In some cases, the source of these issues lies within the resident, while at other times, the focus of concern must be the family, the nursing home, the church and synagogue, or the community.

Concerns for the Resident

Some residents adjust fairly well to their losses and even accept institutionalization as a good option for their care. Ideally, the resident should be an active party in the decision to enter the nursing home. At times, however, residents will experience intense feelings of anger, frustration, and even guilt over their losses and the ensuing institutionalization. Every resident struggles with the question, why is this happening to me? Depression, withdrawal, and resignation may be the ultimate result. It is normal for residents to experience these feelings, especially within the first few months of living in the nursing home. For some, these feelings intensify over time, leaving the resident feeling hostile and abandoned by God, his family, and society. Fears about the future may also be part of this feeling, particularly when the resident feels he or she has little or nothing positive left in life. This is an especially acute problem for residents who are relatively well functioning when they are surrounded by crippled and disfigured residents with little ability to care for themselves. Finding a way to put these experiences into a meaningful perspective and maintain hope for the future is vital to the spiritual well-being of these residents.

Concerns of the Families of Residents

Families react to the institutionalization of their relatives in very different ways. Some work with the resident to arrive at the decision to enter a nursing home and support a smooth

Chart 7–1: Needs of Elderly in Nursing Homes

Physical Needs

_____ to receive an accurate diagnosis of condition and appropriate health care

_____ to be cared for in a sensitive and humane manner

_____ to live in a clean and sanitary environment

_____ to be free from physical and chemical abuse

_____ to have an opportunity for adequate physical exercise

_____ to be provided with special equipment and supplies to increase physical capacities and comfort

Psychological Needs

_____ to remain in control of decisions affecting one's life style and care

_____ to be given support in adjusting to the nursing home environment

_____ to be given support in dealing with depression, stress, and family conflicts

_____ to be given support in adjusting to disorders and impairments

_____ to be free of psychological abuse

Social Needs

_____ to maintain contact with one's family, friends, and other important social groups, including one's church or synagogue

_____ to overcome social isolation and neglect

_____ to be provided with opportunities to engage in meaningful social activities

_____ to have opportunities to do things which are fun and challenging

_____ to be part of a caring community within the nursing home

Spiritual Needs

_____ to be provided opportunities to practice one's faith in accordance with personal traditions

_____ to be given opportunities to discuss religious questions, concerns, and issues with individuals who can help in addressing these concerns

_____ to remain part of one's community of faith, both participating in activities as fully as possible and making contributions to one's church or synagogue

transition to life in the nursing home. Many families regularly visit their institutionalized relatives and are able to maintain a very satisfying relationship with them. At other times, however, the family is not able to accept the impairments of their older relatives. It is very difficult for families to adjust to major physical or psychological changes in parents or spouses. Further, to watch the slow decline of a loved one is extremely painful.

Understanding and accepting this process can be as difficult for the family as it is for the resident. Families may feel intense guilt at having to place their relative in a nursing home. Many do their best to care for their impaired relatives themselves, feeling that placing a family member in a nursing home is a terrible act and a sign of failure. This creates a great deal of stress within the family. Some families react to this stress by avoiding contact with their relative once he or she is placed in a nursing home. Others visit constantly and often attempt to provide a great deal of care for them. At one extreme, the family may continue to treat their relative as if he or she were very sick or impaired, in spite of a leveling off or improvement in the older person's condition. This need to see the older relative as being very sick is part of the family's justification for its needs to keep its older relative in the nursing home. This obviously can have negative effects on the resident, since being sick and dependent is being reinforced by the family, rather than functioning at his or her highest level. In all of these cases, the resident's family may need help in dealing with guilt, setting reasonable visiting patterns, and planning appropriate activities during their visits.

Maintaining good family relationships is an important aspect of the spiritual well-being of residents. Often it is not enough simply to work with the resident but also to understand the resident's family relationships. Once these are understood, work can begin with both the resident and the family to maximize the well-being of the entire family unit.

Concerns Related to the Nursing Home

In an effort to assure quality care, nursing homes are heavily regulated by both state and federal governments and, to a lesser degree, county and municipal governments. Standards for licensure are set by state governments, although certification criteria for a skilled or intermediate care facility is provided by the federal government. Periodic inspections are the primary means by which regulatory agencies determine if a nursing home is meeting standards for care. However, considerable criticism has been directed toward both the regulating agencies and nursing home operators about poor inspection procedures and fraud (see, for example, Mendelson, 1974; Moss and Halmandaris, 1977; Townsend, 1971, and Vladek, 1980). Horror stories are common which cite unsanitary conditions, neglect, and abuse of patients, which can include physical, chemical, and psychological abuse. Denial of the right to practice one's faith and of protection from proselytization are also problems in many nursing homes. Unfortunately, these are grim realities in far too many homes.

Even homes which abide by high standards of operation may take actions which undermine their residents' spiritual well-being. A clean building and well-executed medical procedures are simply not enough to assure quality of life for residents. Rigid operating procedures and schedules often do not allow for flexible responses to the needs of individuals. For example, a well-planned activity program is important in a nursing home, but, if it does not offer a wide range of options which are tailored to the needs of all the residents, it will not meet the needs of each individual. Ideally, residents should be provided with a range of options and adequate time to pursue their interests at a pace that is appropriate for each individual.

In effect, the institutional routines often take away an individual residents' right to decide how to live his or her own life. A constant tension exists in a nursing home between respecting the very personal needs of individual residents and the need for order and smooth operating procedures within the institution. Limited finances and constraints on staff time add to this problem. Even in the best of facilities, there is often not enough time or resources to provide the range of options and flexible schedules that would be preferred by residents.

Concerns in Maintaining Community Support

Communitywide support and involvement with a nursing home is essential for the well-being of residents. Even when families and nursing home staff do their best, ties to the larger community are necessary to help residents maintain contact with the world outside the nursing home. This gives residents an opportunity to remain in touch with their past, as well as keep abreast of the present. Further, most nursing home residents maintain their full rights of citizenship. Many are fully capable of participating in community events ranging from voting in elections to attending parades and concerts. Programs at senior centers, libraries, schools, and park districts may be of special interest to nursing home residents, if the residents are provided with a chance to participate in these activities.

Interaction with people of all ages, including young children, is important for residents. Further, opportunities to engage in everyday activities, such as shopping, going to a movie, or eating at a restaurant, often have very special meaning for those who live in a nursing home. Participation in these activities helps to combat fears about being isolated and different from everyone else in the community. It also gives community residents an opportunity to see and interact with older people who live in nursing homes. When managed properly, these activities can break down many of the stereotypes about nursing home residents.

Unfortunately, not all residents are able to leave the nursing home. Both local and national events should be discussed in the nursing home, and opportunities to participate in activities such as voting should be extended to residents. Community groups, ranging from school children to church groups, should be encouraged to share their activities with residents on an ongoing basis. Residents, in turn, can share their knowledge and experience with these groups. A two-way process of sharing can be initiated, with residents maintaining involvement in the community and the community becoming active in the nursing home. Not only will this enhance the spiritual well-being of nursing home residents, but it will also open up an opportunity for the community to tap a valuable resource, that is, the elderly living in their community.

Concerns of Churches and Synagogues

An essential kind of community involvement is with churches and synagogues. A holistic orientation necessitates that spiritual well-being be included within all the previously mentioned kinds of community activities and involvement with nursing home residents. Particularly for those residents who have been active in church or synagogue, maintaining involvement is indeed very important! This is a topic we will return to in a few pages.

Current Programming in Nursing Homes

Nursing homes vary greatly in the extent to which they encourage and support program development. Some attempt to develop a wide range of programs which enrich the lives of residents and open the nursing home to the community. Other homes remain guarded, closed off, and devoid of meaningful programs for residents.

There are relatively few public or private programs which have been established for the sole purpose of meeting the needs of nursing home residents. The role of the government (including federal, state, and local governments) is largely limited to setting standards and enforcing relations, as well as offering financial assistance to residents through such programs as Medicaid, Medicare, and Social Security. These functions clearly have an impact on the quality of residents' lives; however, the focus of these government activities tends to be on insuring adequate minimum standards for care rather than providing for the well-being of residents. Individual nursing homes are left to their own devices when they go beyond providing for the very basic needs of nursing home residents.

Within nursing homes, responsibliity for program development is shared among several different people. The administrator is ultimately responsible for all programming, but generally this responsibility is delegated to other staff members. Often the activity director and activity staff are given the primary responsibility for developing the social and recreational programs. Frequently, this includes the religious program sponsored by the home. A social worker and social service designee may also design programs to address social and psychological needs of residents. Some nursing homes also have a chaplain or part-time rabbi or coordinator of religious activities who is primarily responsible for religious programming and responding to the spiritual needs of residents. Different individuals on the nursing staff are also involved in designing programs, particularly those related to the physical care and therapeutic needs of residents.

While many staff members participate in coordinating programs for the care of nursing home residents, the activity director and staff are among the most accessible to church and synagogue groups. Not only does this staff typically develop and coordinate the nursing home's social, recreational, and religious activities, but it often assumes responsibility for actually leading the programs. Frequently, the activity department looks to volunteers for assistance, particularly in the areas of planning and leading activities.

Perhaps most common among the volunatry organizations which assist in program development are community and church-sponsored and synagogue-sponsored groups. Among these are youth and children's groups, school-sponsored groups, the Boy Scouts, Girl Scouts, women's groups, garden clubs, circles, sisterhoods, men's organizations, choirs, musical groups, outreach ministries, fraternal groups, and civic organizations. Some of these groups sponsor activities which take place on a daily or weekly basis, while others provide monthly or seasonal activities. In facilities with minimal staffing in the activities department, it is only through the commitment of volunteers that any substantial form of life-enriching programming is brought to residents.

Some facilities encourage residents to assume an active role in programming. Residents may become involved in informal discussions about programs and may give their input in this manner. Other facilities encourage the development of resident councils as formally organized decision-making groups. Resident councils can serve a variety of functions, from mediating problems to making recommendations on policies, and procedures, and the development of meaningful programs. While often difficult to organize, these groups can provide an excellent mechanism for increasing the role of residents in developing and leading programs.

The range of activities which can be shared with nursing home residents is limited only by the imagination of those developing the programs. A list of program ideas has been compiled and is presented at the end of this chapter. The list can be used to suggest ideas for programs, as well as a springboard for developing new ideas.

The Role of the Church and Synagogue

Churches and synagogues have traditionally provided nursing home residents with opportunities to observe their faith by sponsoring worship services and visitation in homes. In some states, such as Illinois, nursing homes are actually required by law to assure that their residents have an opportunity to practice their faith. To better understand the types of religious activities which are currently being provided in nursing homes, our staff initiated a study of seventy one nursing homes in the Chicago metropolitan area. As part of this survey, a staff person at twenty of these nursing homes was questioned about their religious programming. The results indicate some interesting trends in programming, as well as raise some important issues which should be considered in developing new programs.

We learned through our survey that nearly all nursing homes provided some type of regular religious programming. Only one of the twenty homes had no religious programming. On the average, these nursing homes provided four to five religious programs which were held on a weekly, biweekly, monthly, or seasonal basis. Many homes offered services for residents of differing denominational backgrounds, including Roman Catholic, Protestant, and Jewish services. Community clergy led these services in 75 percent of the homes, with nursing home staff and lay people occasionally leading services. Residents rarely participated in leading their religious services. Clergy made regular visits to residents in three-fourths of these homes. As shown in Table 7–1, however, only about half of the homes provided special holiday programs, as well as Bible studies for residents.

Special Issues in Developing Church-Sponsored Programs in Nursing Homes

While we were impressed by the fact that many churches and synagogues are providing a variety of programs in nursing homes, the study also raised some concerns about how

Table 7–1
Religious Programs Available in Selected Nursing Homes

(Percent of nursing homes offering each type of religious program. N = 20.)

Type of Program	Percent
Religious Services	95.0%
Roman Catholic	(80.0%)
Protestant	(70.0%)
Jewish	(20.0%)
Ecumenical	(15.0%)
Other	(35.0%)
Visitation by Clergy	75.0%
Seasonal Holiday Program	55.0%
Bible Studies	45.0%
Other Special Programs	30.0%
Religous Sing-a-longs	30.0%
Communion	20.0%
Invitation to services or programs in community churches	20.0%
Other prayer services or meetings	10.0%
No organized religious programs	5.0%
No response	5.0%

adequately the spiritual needs of residents are being met. First, we have concerns about the quality and appropriateness of religious programs offered in nursing homes. A poorly organized and weak program is quite ineffective at meeting spiritual needs. Second, it was very difficult to judge whether or not the programs we identified were properly matched to the needs and interests of the residents. It is important that all residents be given an opportunity to observe religious practices which are part of their belief system and religious heritage. Yet, not all homes mentioned programs which were designed for residents of all denominations, including Roman Catholics, the full range of Protestant denominations, and Jews. While it is true that some homes do not have residents from all of these denominations, one would expect to find a mix of services in all except homes which restrict their intake to a narrowly defined religious group.

Further, we found that many homes provide ecumenical worship services or a single Protestant service to meet the needs of many of their residents. These services were not always accompanied by additional services for specific Protestant denominations, Roman Catholics, and Jews. This approach to programming creates a variety of problems. A single ecumenical service or generic Protestant service rarely is able to meet the needs of all residents. It simply does not allow residents an opportunity to worship in a manner that is consistent with their denominational guidelines and traditions. Even homes which provide Protestant, Catholic, and Jewish services must continue to struggle with matching these services to the needs of residents. Frequently, individuals from a similar denominational background interpret their faith differently or observe strikingly different traditions. Spiritual concerns are deeply personal and highly individualized. Not all Protestants will enjoy the same Protestant services. Nor will all Catholics be satisfied with the same mass or all Jews accept the same "Kiddush" service. A sensitive response to spiritual needs requires providing each resident with a range of options for worship and allowing the resident to choose to participate in observances which are most consistent with his or her personal faith system and religious traditions.

Making available a wide range of options in worship means more than providing several different types of worship services. The list of programs presented in Table 4-1, in Chapter 4, suggests a diversity of programs designed to address spiritual needs which it is possible to develop in the nursing home. Opportunities to participate in group prayer services, choirs, or musical groups and study groups are of interest to some residents. Regularly receiving the sacraments is important to most Christian residents, while other ritual observances are important to Jewish residents. Special worship services which are planned to fall on the high holy day are terribly important for residents, yet special holiday services are not held in all nursing homes.

More individualized programs can be of great value to residents. Visitation and distribution of the sacraments are the most common of these individualized programs. For many residents these provide an extremely important opportunity to address their spiritual issues and needs, as well as to observe important religious practices. A variety of other programs may be developed, ranging from a pastoral counseling program to a telephone or card ministry. Allowing residents time and a private place for prayer and mediation is also very important.

As stressed earlier, some nursing home residents are willing and able to remain actively involved in a community church or synagogue. Attending services and other church programs in the community is of great interest to some residents who are able to regularly leave the nursing home. For residents who cannot regularly attend services in the community, programs similar to those for the homebound are particularly appropriate. Sharing literature from the church or synagogue, tape recordings of services, and individualized ministries all hold possibilities for nursing home programs. In addition, some nursing home residents may be able to assist with special service projects and ministries for their religious institutions, from preparing mailings to making telephone contacts to conducting Bible study or prayer groups for the church or synagogue.

Actively involving seniors in planning the response to their individual spiritual needs, as well as preparing group programs, would be one means of developing programs that are more responsive to resident's needs. Our data suggest that residents are rarely involved in leading religious programs or responding to requests for assistance with spiritual matters. Giving residents an active role in planning and leading religious activities holds the potential of enhancing the meaningfulness of these activities, as well as the self-esteem of the residents.

New Directions in Program Development With Nursing Home Residents

When a problem or gap in services is identified at the nursing home, religious groups have several options in choosing how to proceed. The course of action taken by the group should be determined by the type of problem. One type of problem which may be encountered includes violation of basic operating standards or violation of residents' basic rights. For example, an unsanitary home or one with inadequate staffing may be in violation of basic operating standards. As previously mentioned, operating standards are set by state governments with state departments of public health charged with the responsibility of monitoring compliance with these standards. Residents' rights are also established by state laws and specify the personal rights of all nursing home residents. When a religious group observes violations of basic operating standards or residents' rights, it needs to serve as an advocate for residents. The goal of advocacy is to rectify problems or injustices within nursing homes. In some cases, residents can be directly involved in advocacy efforts, while in others an advocate works on behalf of the resident. In either case, advocacy is a service for residents which helps assure that they are provided a reasonable quality of care and allowed to live with dignity.

Usually, the desired outcome of advocacy is a change of policy or operating procedures within errant nursing homes.

Advocacy on behalf of individual residents typically begins with efforts to work out a problem with the nursing home staff. It may, however, escalate to taking legal action against the home to insure that it provides for residents in a manner which conforms to the law. Other forms of advocacy include legislative efforts aimed at nursing home reform.

A second type of problem relates to improving the care and quality of life within the home but does not include violation of operating procedures or residents' rights. Often this type of problem can be addressed by working with residents and staff to develop needed programs. Returning to the list of needs, it is possible to identify a number of programs which could be developed by churches or synagogues to meet some of these needs, as shown in Chart 7–2.

Obviously, this list is illustrative of the range of programs which are possible to develop. No church or synagogue would attempt to provide all these services but, instead, would select one or two types of programs to sponsor. At times, however, it is difficult for an individual religious institution to develop even narrowly defined programs due to limitations of resources. In this case, consideration should be given to possible ways of linking with other churches, synagogues, or community groups to provide for residents' needs. Further, collaboration should be considered an option any time a program could be improved or expanded to a more desirable level by a joint effort among several groups.

A third type of problem arises when available nursing home care is determined to be totally inadequate for the needs of many impaired elderly. Rather than use available resources to improve existing services, religious groups may choose to develop alternative forms of care for the impaired elderly. Denominational groups have a long history of developing nursing homes which provide quality care and, more recently, supporting programs which provide community-based care to the impaired elderly. Although individual churches and synagogues rarely have the resources to undertake developing new facilities, they may be able to work with

Chart 7–2
Nursing Home Residents:
Needs and Programmatic Responses

Physical Needs	*Programmatic Response*
Need for physical exercise	Organize games which require physical activities such as a "special olympics."
	Regularly take residents on walks or trips which allow opportunities for exercise.
Need for special supplies	Make or purchase needed supplies such as lap robes, pillows, clothing, adaptive devices, and so forth.
Need for assistance for the nursing staff	Develop a candy striper program.

Psychological Needs	*Programmatic Response*
Need for support for residents in adjusting to the nursing home and dealing with problems such as depression	Develop a counseling program for residents, perhaps as part of a pastoral care program.
Need for support in dealing with family problems	Provide family counseling, peer counseling, and support groups.

Social Needs	*Programmatic Response*
Need for meaningful social activities	Develop a variety of social programs and recreational activities.
Need for service opportunities	Develop special projects for residents.
Need for a sense of community in the nursing home	Plan group activities fostering positive interaction between residents, families, and staff.
Need for community involvement	Develop a transportation and/or escort service which will take residents to church or synagogue, shopping, the library, civic programs, and so forth.

Chart 7–2 (continued)
Nursing Home Residents:
Needs and Programmatic Responses

Spiritual Needs	*Programmatic Response*
Need to participate in worship services	Develop regular religious services or provide transportation for residents to participate in church or synagogue services.
Need for opportunities to discuss spiritual questions and issues	Develop discussion groups, or individual and group spiritual counseling programs.
Need to maintain contact with one's community of faith	Plan to regularly involve residents in church or synagogue activities by bringing these activities into the nursing home or extending invitations for residents to attend church or synagogue activities.

their respective denominations or associations to fill the gaps in service by providing quality institutional or home-based care for the imparied elderly. Once again a collaborative approach may be possible, drawing on the resources of a number of church or synagogue-related groups and community groups.

Maintaining a Holistic Orientation in Programming

The importance of a holistic orientation in care is nowhere more apparent than in the nursing home. The interaction of the physical, psychological, social, and spiritual dimensions of the person are clear. Residents can be observed who are in poor health but function very well, due to their excellent psychological, social, and spiritual adjustments to their physical problems. Conversely, there are residents in relatively good health who literally cannot care for themselves because of deep depression, social isolation, and withdrawal. Programs which are designed primarily to address one dimension of a resident's needs also have implications for all other dimensions. For example, attending group worship services in nursing homes provides not only an opportunity to address spiritual needs but gives a resident physical exercise in getting to the service, psychological support in dealing with such feelings as anger and frustration, and social interaction with others attending the services.

Efforts to address all these dimensions can be enhanced by understanding the broad treatment implications of a relatively simple activity such as attending a religious service. Simple actions, such as encouraging interaction between residents before and after the service or inviting families to attend services with the residents, increase the social value of these activities. Praise from the clergy, after a long and difficult effort by a physically impaired resident to walk to a service, is extremely helpful in supporting physical therapy. Common psychological problems can be identified and addressed either individually or on an educational level as part of a sermon or small group discussion.

When activities are planned with nursing home residents, it is important to consider the ways in which a program addresses a variety of needs for residents. In order to do this effectively, efforts should be made to understand as much as possible about a resident's physical, psychological, social, and spiritual background. When unusual behaviors or sudden changes are observed in a resident, it is important to report these incidents and try to understand what is happening. Working together, the nursing home staff—including nurses, activity workers, the social worker, and chaplain—can combine efforts with the community clergy or lay volunteers to serve residents in the most appropriate manner. At times, some advocacy on behalf of the resident is necessary to bring together people from these different service areas, but efforts to do so can be extremely rewarding.

Program Ideas

Many different types of programs are possible to develop in nursing homes. While it is always important to work with residents and staff in a particular home to develop programs which are needed, it is also sometimes useful to consider a wide range of programmatic options.

Programs with religious content encompass general worship services, including services on holidays; special worship services for residents with specific types of impairments, such as cognitive disorders; liturgy planning groups involving residents; prayer and meditation groups; Bible studies; prayer groups; other educational or discussion groups; sacramental and ritual observances; visitation; individual prayer and meditation; pastoral counseling; tapes, records, or films on religious themes; regular sharing of items from worship services or other programs at local churches and synagogues, including tapes of sermons, bulletins, newsletters, flowers, holiday decorations, and so forth; escorts for residents to worship services and programs at local churches or synagogues; special programs or luncheons at local churches and synagogues which include nursing home residents; invitations for nursing home residents to participate in circles, friendship clubs, sisterhood and men's groups, and so on. Groups may be formed in the nursing home. Residents may join groups at the church or synagogue. Religious groups may meet periodically at the nursing home. Residents may attend mini-retreats, either intergenerational or only for the elderly.

Programs which may or may not have religious content include friendly visiting; telephone reassurance; adopt-a-Grandparent; adopt-a-Nursing Home; educational or discussion groups on current events or special topics; intergenerational sharing groups; a correspondence or greeting card program; a heritage center arts and crafts, perhaps even directed at developing an art fair or sale; creative writing groups;

games, such as question-and-answer games, board games, cards, and active exercise games; and development of a resident-supported welcoming committee to greet new residents and assist in the adjustment to the facility.

Nursing homes can indeed be bleak environments if not enriched by these kinds of programmatic activities!

Chapter Eight

Living with the Dying

Our focus in this chapter is not on the elderly in a specific setting, such as living in one's own home or in a nursing home. Rather, here we will focus on the elderly who are in the process of dying. Death is one of the few things which is certain in life. It can come at any point in the life span. For the old, however, it is a reality which is often present in day-to-day existence. The death of a spouse and peers, as well as the physical deterioration which accompanies the aging process, are constant reminders of the finite nature of existence.

Death can hold a variety of meanings for both the young and old. In describing attitudes toward death, Shneidman (1973) observed that death is "the most mysterious, the most threatening, and the most tantalizing of all human phenomena" (p. 3). Death is paradoxical: it is both an end and a beginning. It can be feared, yet also accepted, dreaded but welcomed. Death can mean loss, change, conflict, and suffering, but it can also mean triumph (see, for example, Davidson, 1975). It can certainly make life meaningful while being meaningful itself. Each person is challenged to unravel the meaning of death in a highly individualized manner. Attitudes toward life, previous experiences with death, and the specific circumstances surrounding death will shape a person's reaction to a death. Personality factors, as well as religious beliefs, are also extremely important.

Rather than attempt to analyze the meaning of death and dying, the purpose of this chapter is to identify and discuss the needs of older people as they die. Our view is that dying is part of living. As such, it behooves us to be mindful of the needs of older people as they prepare to die and support them in living fully until their death.

Who are the Dying

In one sense, we all are dying: we all are moving closer toward our deaths. Yet, even with a clear assessment of an individual's well-being, it is difficult to predict how close any person is to death. Some who appear to be healthy may die suddenly, whereas others in poor condition may linger on for years. Adding to the difficulty of identifying the dying is the fact that nearness to death may not be openly acknowledged. At times, protective physicians and families may not inform an older person that his or her death is near. Often, this knowledge is shared among family but not with others, including clergy or lay people from one's congregation. This makes it extremely difficult to identify and offer support to the dying.

In the United States in 1981 over two-thirds of the people who died were over the age of sixty-five (U.S. National Center for Health Statistics, 1981). The average life expectancy for children born in 1979 was about seventy-four years, but, if one survived to sixty-five, there was a likelihood of living another twenty years (U.S. Bureau of the Census, 1982). Today death is closely associated with old age which, however, is a rather recent phenomenon. Before the extensive use of antibiotics, death was frequent at all ages. Now death at an early age is actually relatively rare. Advances in medical treatment have extended the average life span so that increasingly people are living into their eighties and nineties. Yet surviving to this very advanced age does not mean that we have lengthened the human life span. Biologists currently estimate the human life span to be, and to have remained at, about 110 to 120 years. As people live out their full life span, however, they do so with biological deterioration, and, if anything, a more lengthy dying process at the end of life. Stated another way, when death comes when one is very old, it is likely to be a prolonged process. Just as all biological systems slow down with age, apparently the dying process does also.

The Needs of the Dying

Human beings are the only creatures known to be aware of their own death. To some theoreticians and theologians, the awareness of death is a core principle of human existence; that is, that one's life can only be understood in the context of the awareness of a limited life span. Because personal death is anticipated, every culture has developed ways of helping its people to cope with the limited nature of existence. In all societies, children are taught about the meaning of death. Further, rituals have been developed to facilitate mourning and to limit an extended mourning process. Belief system and rituals are indispensable for dealing with the apparently innate fear of dying. Thus, all cultures must provide a system of belief to explain death. In some cultures, the meanings revolve around an afterlife. In others, the focus is more on living through one's children and the belief that the family and social institutions that have been left behind will endure following death.

Cultures also vary in the way they define events that are worse than one's personal death. In Oriental societies, for example, loss of face may be more painful than the thought of personal nonexistence. Also, dying to save one's children or dying in defense of one's country has become acceptable for most people in most societies. For the very old, it is not uncommon to wish "not to suffer anymore" and therefore death is welcomed.

In our culture, death is most often perceived as a loss. What is perceived as loss, however, varies from individual to individual. Diggory and Rothman (1961) surveyed people and found that seven kinds of losses were associated with the contemplation of death:

1. Loss of ability to have experiences

2. Loss of ability to predict subsequent events (e.g., life after death)

3. Loss of body and fear of what will happen to the body

4. Loss of ability to care for dependents

5. Loss suffered by friends and family (e.g., causing grief to others)

6. Loss of opportunity to continue plans and projects, and

7. Loss of being in a relatively painless state.

As might be expected, they found that the greatest concern for men was their inability to care for dependents, while the greatest concern for women was causing grief to family and friends. Persons between fifteen and thirty-nine selected causing grief to friends as their major anticipated loss through death, while those over forty chose the inability to care for dependents. A later study by Kalish and Reynolds (1976), in a later study that included more people over fifty-five, reported that caring for dependents was less important for this age group. What was important for the elderly was not a concern with future plans but concerns with having no control over how they will die, concern with not dying alone, and fear of dying with pain.

Death and the Elderly

Munnichs (1966), a social scientist in the Netherlands, has reported that the old are more accepting of their own death than persons of other age groups. This finding, however, was not readily accepted by others. Many felt that, because the elderly are closer to their own death, their fear of dying should be greater. Yet, other studies have supported Munnich's finding, and now it is generally agreed that people in their seventies and eighties begin to accept their own nonexistence.

The fear of death, if anything, is a fear of those in their middle years, and it is often projected onto the very old. Older people in their seventies and eighties are indeed aware of having lived a full life. It is when death occurs at a younger age that people feel that life has been foreshortened; that is, when death is "off-time." It is not uncommon to feel that death at a relatively young age is a punishment for "not having lived a good life." If, however, one lives to old age (for example, age eighty-five) it is assumed that the person has lived a moral life and that old age has been given as a "divine reward." The Book of Proverbs notes, "The fear of the Lord prolongs life but the years of the wicked will be short" (Proverbs 10:27). Thus, it appears that the acceptance of nonbeing among the very old is understandable but that concerns with the way in which death occurs may be very prevalent. To die in a nursing home rather than in one's own home is often dreaded, as is a death when alone or when in great pain. But the fact of death itself apparently does become more acceptable with advanced age. Indeed, this became very evident in the Lieberman and Tobin (1983) study where persons who were closer to death were compared to those who were further from death.

In the Lieberman and Tobin research, a group of older persons (average age seventy-eight) were studied over time. Those who had died in the ensuing two years were compared to those who had continued to live beyond this period. It was found that among those closer to death, there was some level of awareness and a sense of being closer to death. Older people apparently sensed an underlying biological change and generally reacted by becoming somewhat disorganized or constricted in their behaviors. For this reason, a very sensitive nurse who worked in the nursing home in which the study was conducted could detect those who had moved into a terminal phase. Thus, people who are approaching death show signs of being aware that they are dying, although often it is not on a conscious level. Further, they generally do not portray the manifest anxiety regarding impending death that is commonplace among younger people.

The Dying Process

The Lieberman-Tobin study supported the finding of other investigations in which there are systematic changes that take place when death occurs among the very old. These changes have been called either the "death trajectory" or "terminal drop," which refer to systematic changes in behavioral functioning as death approaches. Kubler-Ross (1969) has also discussed a series of specific changes that she considers common to the dying process independent of the age of the person:

> *Stage 1: Denial.* First reactions when aware of impending death may be denial, shock, and disbelief. Denial is a defense which allows an individual time to slowly adjust to the thought of dying.
>
> *Stage 2: Anger.* After a period of denial, the dying individual often becomes angry and asks, "Why me?" Anger is often directed at family, friends, and caregivers.
>
> *Stage 3: Bargaining.* In this stage, the patient wants more time and asks for favors to postpone death. The bargaining may be carried out with the physicain, family, or, more frequently, with God.
>
> *Stage 4: Depression.* Depression is a signal among the young that the dying person has begun to accept impending death. Illness can no longer be denied, as it causes greater weakness and pain.
>
> *Stage 5: Acceptance.* If younger people reach this stage, death is accepted. Although essentially devoid of feeling, he or she wishes to be close to loved ones, but verbal communication may be unnecessary.

suicidal sign

Observations of many other thanatologists confirm the experience of these feelings among the young when they are dying. There is, however, considerable disagreement as to whether or not all dying individuals experience both the full range of feelings described by Kubler-Ross and the specific sequence of stages she detailed, particularly among the old who can more readily accept their own death. Shneidman (1973) suggests an alternative conceptualization to that of Kubler-Ross for death among the young. In his work with younger people who are dying, he has observed that their feelings can be described as a "hive of affect, in which there is a constant coming and going (of feelings)." He further characterized the emotional stages of the dying when young as

> . . . a constant interplay between disbelief and hope and, against these as background, a waxing and waning of anguish, terror, acquiescence and surrender, rage and envy, disinterest and ennui, pretense, taunting and daring and even yearning for death—all in the context of bewilderment and pain. (P. 7)

According to this conceptualization, there is not a single, constant movement through stages but vacillation between acceptance and denial. Kubler-Ross also has cautioned that not all people will experience dying by going through each stage in an orderly fashion.

The value of comparing conceptualizations is that it gives us a slightly different view of the types of feelings any dying person may experience. We must, however, be very careful not to infer that any one of these views presents a portrait of how people die. Each individual faces his or her death in a unique way. There is no simple way to die, much less an ideal way to come to accept death. The person who feels that death is to be "raged against" and does so with his or her last gasp, is actually dying the way in which he or she wished. Another individual may become more resigned and passive, approaching death in a peaceful manner. Stated simply, an appropriate death is dying the way the person chooses, rather than with a sense of equanimity that we as bystanders might wish.

Perhaps, as O'Hare (1982) has discussed, the central question in serving the dying is, what is important *now*? To answer this question, one must be willing to identify the immediate needs of the individual, family, and community and respond to these needs. Careful timing of responses is also important, since many dying individuals often have limited energy to deal with the world around them.

Separating the issues around dying from those of death itself can also be useful for both the dying individual and those providing care. Dying is a physical, psychological, social, and spiritual process. While it is subject to many ups and downs, it is a process which can be coped with and, to some extent, actually managed. Death itself, however, is the final stage of this process, the end of the journey. Fears about death, its unknown aspects, and questions of existence or nonexistence are related but somewhat different from those of the dying process. The thought of death raises broad philosophical, spiritual, and psychological questions. In order to cope with both death and dying, it may be useful, at times, to separate the realities of the dying process from the specter of death itself to more appropriately respond to these concerns as they are raised.

Finally, *caring*, as opposed to simply providing care for the dying, is perhaps one of the most important considerations in working with the dying. No matter what their physical state, dying individuals are feeling human beings. As such, they deserve respect, compassion, and caring.

While spiritual well-being is important throughout life, it is particularly important as one faces death. As previously noted, religious beliefs are important in influencing attitudes toward death for many older people. Further, an individual's understanding of the meaning of both life and death is directly shaped by personal faith. In preparing to die, people usually spend time reflecting on their lives, taking stock of achievements and failures. Being able to find meaning in these experiences, as well as an acceptance of the past, is an important part of preparing to die. Often there is a need for reconciliation—to resolve past conflict with God, community, loved ones, and self. Gaining this sense of reconciliation and resolution can be very important for the dying.

Reaffirmation is also an important concern for the dying. Reaffirmation can take place on spiritual, social, and psychological levels. To reaffirm one's personal faith at the time of death obviously has great meaning for the dying. This opportunity to restate one's faith and find new meaning through faith is a primary source of hope, as well as a means to a deeper personal understanding and acceptance of death. Reaffirmation of important social relationships, particularly with family and close friends, can also be a source of love and personal satisfaction. Finally, reaffirmation of self refers to the recognition that one's identity can remain intact despite the changes which are part of dying. Spiritual reaffirmaion is often central in allowing for reconciliation and reaffirmation on the more social and psychological levels.

Beyond these concerns, a dying individual may require extensive attention to physical needs. As previously emphasized, controlling pain and other noxious physical symptoms is very important. Additionally, the dying may need assistance in completing the tasks of daily living, including providing personal care, meal preparation, and feeding, managing basic household tasks, and transportation. Without assistance in these areas, the dying individual may be forced to use all his or her strength to cope with these routine problems, leaving little physical or psychological energy for other concerns.

Perhaps the greatest concern in working with the dying is to allow each individual the opportunity to adjust and prepare for death in the manner which is best suited for that individual. Individuals must be allowed to control the decisions which are part of dying. If a dying individual cannot express his or her preferences, then doing all possible to respect previously stated wishes is important. People cope with their deaths in a personalized manner which is consistent with their coping patterns throughout life. To ignore this is to deny the dignity of the individual, as well as risk harm to the dying individual. Those caring for the dying should look to them for cues which reflect their needs and preferences, rather than assume what is "best" for dying individuals.

In summarizing the needs of older people as they face death, it is possible, as shown in Chart 8-1, to use the categories of physical, psychological, social, and spiritual needs.

Concerns in Working with the Family of Dying Individuals

As with the dying person, the family needs assistance in coping with the realities of the dying process, as well as grieving the loss of a loved one.

The physical and emotional demands which are part of caring for the dying can be great. In many instances, this job literally ties the family down twenty-four hours of the day. A family can become exhausted and overwhelmed after coping with this stress for extended periods of time. Some families need assistance in providing physical care for the dying individual. Other times, the family can manage the physical care but needs someone to stay with the dying person while the family takes a break from the responsibility of providing care. Families need time for simple tasks, such as shopping and errands, as well as breaks for relaxation. Having someone come to their home one or more days per week can be extremely helpful in managing the stress which is part of caring for a dying individual.

Families often have difficulty setting reasonable limits on what they can and cannot do for a dying relative. Many families feel obligated to provide this care and experience feelings of guilt when they cannot do everything for the dying individual. Helping families set reasonable limits on behavior is often important. To do so may require sorting through guilt, as well as through personal feelings about death and dying. This can be a problem both for families who care for dying relatives at home and for those whose relatives are in institutional settings. At the other extreme, one may encounter families which avoid dying relatives and seem neglectful to those individuals' needs. In such cases, work with the family may involve exploring feelings of denial of death, as well as other sources of conflict between the family members.

Beyond helping families cope with the dying process, they often need support in grieving the loss of their loved ones. Grieving may begin long before an individual's physical death. Grieving family members often experience a flood of confusing and conflicting feelings. These feelings can include guilt, anger, frustration, sorrow, anxiety, and depression. Family members may also experience physical illness or distress which is related to the stress of caring for a dying individual and mourning their loss. Responses can vary widely, from becoming totally preoccupied with the dying or dead individual to seemingly erasing any thought of the person.

It is important to help families understand their grief as a normal reaction to the loss of a loved one. Indeed, the price of forming attachments to others is to mourn their loss when they are gone. The grieving process can be described as having four phases (see, for example, Huyck and Hoyer, 1982).

THE FIRST PHASE. The first response to death is shock, with some denial that the death has actually occurred. There may be a profound sense of unreality. At times, grieving individuals may become very forgetful and disoriented. They may even experience the presence of the dead individual.

THE SECOND PHASE. Next, the person experiences grief. There is a subjective feeling of intense psychic pain. There are strong desires to recover the lost person. In an extreme case, the individual may commit suicide in order to "join the loved one." When the realization occurs that nothing can be done, the sufferer become very withdrawn. Muscles become flaccid. Fatigue, exhaustion, and loss of appetite are common. This stage of grief indicates that the mourner is beginning to sense the reality of the loss.

THE THIRD PHASE. As the person becomes more realistic, a separation reaction occurs. There is now the realization that the dead one is no longer externally present. Anxiety is one response to the danger entailed by the loss. The danger may be realistic threats to security and safety. For example, an

Chart 8–1
Needs of the Dying

Physical Needs
— to receive an accurate diagnosis of condition, with particular sensitivity to the multiple chronic conditions of many elderly
— to be prescribed an individualized treatment system, with a minimum of negative side effects
— to control pain and other noxious disease symptoms
— to have periodic reassessments of condition and appropriate adjustments in treatment
— to receive assistance with activities of daily living, such as walking, bathing, toileting, eating, and the like
— to have care provided in a sensitive and humane manner, with respect of the human being

Psychological Needs
— to be honestly told of their condition in a way which can be tolerated by the dying
— to maintain hope even in very bleak circumstances
— to be supported in talking about death and dying, including expressing the range of feelings, such as denial, anger, rage, frustration, and depression
— to be supported in grieving the many losses which are part of dying
— to be allowed to slowly come to terms with death in an individualized manner
— to be treated with dignity and allowed to remain in control of decisions about one's life, including efforts to preserve one's life

Social Needs
— to maintain relationships with family, friends, and loved ones which share love and affection
— to maintain contact with social groups which have been important to the individual
— to have someone to talk with and share thoughts and feelings which are encountered in the dying process
— to resolve conflicts, particularly with loved ones
— to make plans for one's funeral, finalize personal matters, and dispose of one's belongings

Chart 8–1 (continued)
Needs of the Dying

— to receive assistant with a variety of tasks, such as cooking, cleaning, transportation, running errands and the like, as needed
— to say goodbye when the appropriate time arrives

Spiritual Needs
— to openly discuss religious questions, issues, and concerns
— to be given the opportunity to reaffirm one's faith as death approaches
— to participate in religious ceremonies and rituals which are particularly appropriate as the time of death approaches
— to remain part of the community of faith

older man may be anxious about who will care for him if he cannot walk, shop, or get to the doctor alone. His wife, who is now dead, may have made it possible for him to stay out of an institution. In addition to missing the trusted person, there may be feelings of anger at being left alone to endure the pain of that loss. Other common responses are guilt, remorse, and self-accusation. Guilt may lead to an idealization of the dead. Lopata (1973) has found that many widows idealize their late husbands as a way of dealing with any negative feelings they may have had.

THE FOURTH PHASE. The reorganization phase begins the recovery process. An important part of reorganization is identification with the lost person. The mourner may take on the mannerisms, habits, conversational style, concerns, and even the illness of the deceased. Such behavior "gives comfort to the mourner, makes them feel close to the deceased and thus mitigates somewhat the pain of loss" (Pinkus, 1976). Through identification, the lost person becomes part of the self. The dead person is internalized; in this way, he or she cannot be lost. The survivor has changed to incorporate the beloved. Identification thus represents a filling up or a replenishing of the self in order to become a stronger, better-integrated, or separate person. As this occurs, the reality and finality of the external loss is accepted.

These stages of the grieving process serve as guides for understanding the process, rather than as rigid rules for mourning. Generally, families work through this process in a healthy manner, especially when they receive support. It is important, however, to watch for extreme reactions to the loss of a loved one. In some cases, professional help is warranted.

Community Services for the Dying

Death is a process which can take place in a variety of settings. Increasingly, hospitals and other institutions are the locations in which people die. Yet, with the broadening range of health care options, there are a variety of means to care for the dying.

Hospitals are among the first places many individuals with life-threatening conditions turn to for care. Generally, hospitals provide treatment for acute conditions, as well as emergency care. Although hospitals at times may provide extended care for the terminally ill, their emphasis is usually curative. The aim of curative care is to stop the disease process and, to the extent possible, restore healthy functioning.

Hospices provide an alternative form of care for the dying. Emphasis is placed on making the patient comfortable and controlling pain, as well as providing emotional and spiritual support. Extraordinary life support systems are not used in hospice programs. This is referred to as palliative, rather than curative, care.

Nursing homes can also provide twenty-four hour care for the dying, particularly those with chronic conditions or slowly degenerative illnesses. The type of care available in nursing homes varies widely, from being curative or palliative care to being custodial care.

In some cases, the elderly choose to live out their lives in their homes. Some do not need extensive medical care.

Others have families, friends, or other willing individuals who are available to meet the needs of the older person who wishes to die at home. Home-health care agencies are a very important resource for individuals dying at home. Services which can be provided range from skilled nurses able to supervise complex medical treatments to in-home companions and housekeepers. Many hospice groups are available to provide support in individual's homes, as well as in institutional settings.

The hospice movement is of increasing importance in setting standards for care of the dying. Dr. Cecily Saunders (1969) developed the first hospice in England because she believed that the terminally ill should be supported in seeking a satisfactory death in an environment where they could comfortably say their goodbyes to those left behind. The hospice was a facility that did not function like a hospital. Medication was given to relieve pain, but emphasis was placed on keeping the person lucid so that there could be interaction with the family and friends. Saunders's ideal patient was a woman in her early thirties with cancer who was saying goodbye to her husband and children. Support provided at the hospice helped the family feel that their lives would go on satisfactorily after the patient's departure. This concept has now been brought into the United States and been expanded to include the elderly. Emphasis has been shifted to include provision of terminal care in people's homes.

Indeed, in our small study, we found that the main thrust of hospices in the Chicago area was on terminal care in the home. Moreover, many of the dying patients were very old. This is consistent with the national trend toward increasing hospice care for the very old. Hospice care, of course, is also a cost-saving mechanism because the elderly can be cared for in hospices at less cost than in a typical hospital bed. This aspect notwithstanding, this specialized caring, whether in a hospice facility or at home, offers a great improvement in direct care to the dying.

Our study also found that hospices are a way of enhancing the collaboration of physicians, clergy, and social service personnel. Through collaboration, not only are roles defined for each profession group but an important principle emerges: that whatever is done must be guided by the beliefs and wishes of the dying patient and his or her family.

The Role of the Church or Synagogue

Churches and synagogues have a long history of responding to the needs of the dying. Clergy are among the first who are called to attend to the dying and their families. Religious rituals have been long associated with preparing to die, as well as mourning a loss.

New Directions for Program Development for Church and Synagogue

It is possible to define four broad ways in which church and synagogue can support the dying and their families. The first area is perhaps the most familiar, that is, offering spiritual and emotional support and guidance. Visitation to the hospitalized and homebound frequently includes visits to the dying. Pastoral counseling is also extended to these individuals. Support groups for dying individuals and their families are another example of programs which offer spiritual and emotional support to the dying. The purpose of all these programs is to reach out to those struggling to understand and accept death and remind them that they are part of a larger, supportive community.

A second way in which religious groups can be supportive of the dying is to offer assistance in meeting an individual's physical needs and performing tasks which are necessary to provide for his or her care. Providing direct physical care can be extremely demanding for families. Additionally, maintaining a household and running errands can take a great deal of time. As previously mentioned, families often need assistance with these tasks. Further, the cost of special care and equipment can be high. While insurance is helpful with many medical bills and major equipment, many smaller, disposable items are not paid for by insurance. Financial assistance, as well as support in identifying where and how to obtain needed supplies, is often useful. Sometimes, just having someone make telephone calls to agencies which provide the needed services and supplies is very helpful. Respite care is also very important. This refers to providing someone to relieve the family of caretaking responsibility to allow family members a break from the pressures of caring for the dying individual.

A third role the church and synagogue can play in assisting the dying and their families is to help in actually planning for the death. Although planning for death occurs thoughout life, it can be systematized in a way that is supportive for both the dying and their families. For example, the Lutheran Brotherhood (1975) has published a brochure that includes most of the important questions to be dealt with when facing death.

1. Do you wish heroic measures and/or artificial means to be used to sustain you life?

2. Who should be notified at the time of your death (family, funeral home, friends, employers, cemetery, unions, fraternal and professional organizations, Social Security office, attorney, insurance agencies, and so on)?

3. What kind of funeral service do you want?

4. Where should the service be held?

5. Do you wish a burial or cremation?

6. Do you wish to prepurchase a cemetary lot? Where?

7. Do you wish a grave marker? What should it say?

8. Do you wish to donate any of your bodily parts for medical research or training?

9. Do you wish to permit autopsy if requested by the hospital? What special arrangements should be made if you die away from home?

While this list was developed for use with survivors to facilitate their planning process, it obviously can be used to help a dying individual consider questions relevant to his or her dying process and wishes about observances after death.

The fourth major area in which churches and synagogues can be helpful is by working with grieving families after the death of their loved one. Religious rituals are particularly important in facilitating the mourning process. Funeral services, wakes, and the Jewish ritual of "sitting shiva," where family and friends gather to support the bereaved, are particularly important. In addition, if it is understood that the mourning process takes time and occurs in sequence, that information can be helpful in assuring a satisfactory outcome. Obviously, the relationship between the dying person and the bereaved survivor will determine the process and its resolution. For the spouse who is overburdened with caregiving, there may be a mixture of relief and grief. There often will be the feeling that life cannot be structured adequately without the presence of the lost spouse. The attitude of children will also vary. If children perceive the parents as having lived a full life, they may be better able to accept death. The loss of the second parent has a special meaning to the surviving children. No longer is their parent between themselves and their maker. Often the children who lose a second parent feel like orphans, abandoned and closer to their own deaths.

While rituals are very significant, it is also important to remember that the grieving process can take a considerable amount of time and become manifest in various ways. It can take many months, even years, to fully resolve the loss of a loved one. Some grieving family members can benefit from various forms of support which extend beyond the first weeks after the death of their loved one. Visitation, counseling, and support groups can all be helpful. Further, some survivors need help untangling complex financial and legal problems in settling the affairs of the deceased. The church and synagogue can be very helpful in addressing all these concerns.

Churches and synagogues often work with the dying on very individualized and personalized bases through their pastoral care programs. Clearly, it is also possible to develop more formalized intervention for the dying and their families. Counseling and support groups can be structured in either formal or informal manners, as can programs designed to provide physical and financial assistance to the dying. Further, it is possible for churches and synagogues to either sponsor a hospice program or provide volunteer and financial assistance to these programs. Congregations can also coordinate their supportive efforts with agencies, such as home-health groups, to enhance the services available to dying individuals. These ideas suggest the wide range of options in providing support for the dying.

Program Ideas

The program ideas suggested in Chapter 6 and 7, which focused upon serving the homebound and nursing home residents, provide useful references for ideas on programming for the dying. The nature of the setting and the needs of the individuals caring for the dying both shape the type of programmatic response which is appropriate. Flexibility and the ability to respond quickly as needs arise are the hallmarks of good programs for the dying. Once again, a holistic orientation is essential. Among the program ideas which may be useful are support programs for the dying, including those that provide emotional and spiritual support; provide assistance with the physical care and tasks of daily living; coordinate activities and supplement support from community agencies, including home-health agencies; provide financial assistance to purchase needed care or supplies; include work with others to develop and support hospice programs; and provide legal assistance when possible. Needed also are support programs for relatives and friends of the dying, such as respite care that is available to the family of the dying person; support groups for widows, widowers, and family members, as well as other groups of people resolving the loss of a loved one; individual support and counseling for the survivors; outreach programs for the grieving to include them in activities of the congregation and community; concrete assistance with tasks of daily living for the survivors, as appropriate; and appropriate experts available to assist with complex legal and financial questions. Also educational activities about the dying process are needed within the congregation, such as discussing the medical, legal, and financial aspects of this process; bringing speakers into the congregation and community to help people understand the dying process and help individuals reach a satisfactory acceptance of their own death; sponsoring activities which help individuals plan for their own death; and conducting congregational "Confirmation of Death" seminars in which individuals are helped to face their own death in a meaningful way, so as to make their current life more meaningful (see, in particular, Schmitt, 1967, and Davidson, 1975).

Clearly, the dying elderly and their families are a group that can uniquely benefit from the activities of religious institutions. In turn, a holistic approach to their spiritual well-being facilitates the development of a wealth of initiatives that can have special meaning to those who are undergoing the final stage of life, as well as those loved ones who will be left behind.

Part III

Religious Institutions and the Service System

Throughout this book, we have noted the importance of working together on behalf of the elderly. This is not an easy task. In Chapter 9, Working Together, we discuss the benefits as well as the obstacles, that churches and synagogues confront in working with the other congregations and social service agencies. The focus of this chapter is on the discussion of the various approaches to working together. In Chapter 10, A Model for Increasing Interaction Among Churches, Synagogues, and Social Agencies, we discuss our own model that was developed to facilitate the enhancement of cooperation between churches and synagogues and social agencies.

Chapter Nine

Working Together

T ry as they might, most churches and synagogues find that they can not respond to all the needs of the elderly. Indeed, they need not do so. As a result of various federal, state, and local initiatives, agencies are providing for everything from food and shelter to counseling for the elderly. Many communities, however, do not have the necessary resources to meet all of the needs of their aged. As we have noted in earlier chapters, when considering initiating a program for the elderly, a church or synagogue should begin the planning process by contacting local social service agencies to find out what they are providing. During the initial contact, there should be some discussion of possible ways to work together. Working together improves our ability to meet the needs of the whole person, making it more likely that gaps in services will be identified, that unnecessary duplication will be avoided, that existing services will be more fully used, and that useful news services will be developed. In this chapter, we will examine some of the possible approaches to working together in the local community.

Reasons for Working Together

Working together is not a new idea. Several years ago, Breckenridge, et al. (1952), discussed the importance of collaborative efforts among churches and other community agencies. Further, Beattie (1963) reported on a project in which a welfare council worked with churches to identify methods and guidelines for churches to use in developing programs for the aging. Numerous studies have verified that working together has some real benefits for both the service providers and the elderly receiving the services (see, for example, Rossi, Gilmartin and Dayton, 1982). Some of the possible benefits are as follows:

1. Working together allows the various groups to pool their financial and human resources to their mutual benefit.

2. Working together allows the gifts of each group to be shared. While one church or synagogue may have the expertise to develop a senior club, they may need the meeting room of the other.

3. Working together can insure adequate numbers of participants in programs. Sometimes a smaller church encounters a need but finds that there are not enough people who have the need to justify developing a program. For example, one church may realize that they have six people that could benefit from a discussion group for widows. However, without the seven people from the synagogue next door, they would not have enough people to justify developing the group or to make it run smoothly.

4. Working with a local social service agency may provide the expertise to run a program well. Often local social agencies have people who have studied the needs of the elderly and learned from the experiences of others how to provide programs. Working with their guidance can prevent duplicating the mistakes of others.

5. Working with local religious organizations and social service agencies can provide greater access to the people who are in need. Because churches and synagogues are community institutions that do not have the stigma of social service or mental

health agencies, they are often able to identify and reach out to people who might otherwise fail to seek help for their problems.

6. Working together allows agencies, churches, and synagogues to assess the types of services that are not available in the community and to work together to provide them.

7. Working together facilitates making referrals between groups. Studies (see, for example, Veroff, Kulka and Douvan, 1981) consistently have shown that elderly with a social service need turn first to their minister, priest, or rabbi for assistance. This places clergy in a position of being able to refer their parishioners to a local social service agency when the church or synagogue is not able to respond to the need.

Barriers to Working Together

While we believe that it is important to work together to provide services for the elderly, we are also aware of some of the problems in establishing these working relationships. Stone and Garner (1981) observed, "Traditionally, ministers and mental health professionals encounter difficulty communicating with one another. Each tends to distrust the other and view the other's understanding of humanity as incompatible with his or her own" (p. 246).

While some communities seem to find working together easily accomplished, many do not. Steinitz (1980), in her study of the churches and social service agencies in one community, found that clergy and human social service personnel rarely collaborated in service provision to the elderly, even though they often worked with the same people. In this study, she quotes (on pages 138 and 139) comments from administrators of social service agencies about churches:

"My mind doesn't include churches." (Director, Commission on Aging)

"Contacts with churches are, at best, incidental. We don't think about them." (Director, Senior Adult Recreation Center)

"No one on our staff is very religious (i.e., goes to church) . . . don't include churches in our work with seniors." (Attorney Senior's Project, Legal Assistance Foundation)

The clergy express similar feelings about social service agencies:

"I hardly ever get asked about agencies in the community." (Minister, Methodist Church)

"I've learned about nursing homes in the area only because that's what people ask me about. Our congregants don't need the other services. I don't know specifics about them." (Rabbi, Reform Synagogue)

"I (only) know about General Assistance (of all agencies in town) because one of our members works there . . . If I have any question, I'll ask her." (Minister, Christian Methodist Episcopal Church)

At best, Steinitz suggests that the clergy and social service agency directors know very little about each other. Clearly, this can be dysfunctional for the elderly. For example, there are times when it is appropriate to refer an elderly person to a pastor or rabbi for counseling, and also there are times when the elderly person should be referred to a social agency.

Possibly the greatest barrier to working together is a lack of communications which results in many misconceptions about each other. Unfortunately, work demands of clergy and social service agency personnel make it difficult to spend the necessary time for appropriate introductions. A most common communication link between religious groups and social service agencies is the social agency worker who is a member of a local church or synagogue. Yet, the "religious" social worker is generally unable to provide enough communication to bridge the gaps between these two types of insititutions (Ellor, 1983).

"Turf issues" are another common obstacle in increasing interaction. When there are rigid understandings about the limits on the role of each community group, it is very difficult to encourage collaboration. Often competition between groups, old rivalries, and jealous protection of one's turf underlie these disputes. These conflicts tend to divide rather than unify the community.

At times the attitudes and personality of the professionals interfere. In one community we studied, the only major community social service agency for the elderly was directed by a person who wanted everyone to work together but to do it only that agency's way. Although clergy felt working with that agency could be helpful to the needs of their aged, they had so many negative encounters with the director that they were unwilling to do so. While we would like to believe that the personality of professionals is not a factor in any consideration of working together, in reality, it can be a significant problem.

Finally, we found examples where working together was inhibited because of differences in values. Clergy who do not believe in abortion do not send anyone to social service agencies that condone abortions. In one community, clergy at opposite ends of the theological scale were the ones most opposed to working together. At one extreme, the conservative or fundamentalist Christian clergy felt that Jesus was the answer to everything and that even the other churches would not understand this enough to justify working with them. At the other extreme, the Unitarian Universalists found it difficult to work with some other churches because they continually discussed God, and God is not a necessary part of the Unitarian philosophy. In like manner, Jewish Orthodox and Reform congregations may find it difficult to work together.

Service personnel, in turn, often believe that guilt causes undue anguish and perceive clergy as inducing guilt. Numerous examples of these phenomenon can be given. Clearly, each church, synagogue, and social service agency feels justified in its position, yet the potential for their seniors to miss out on the benefits of collaborative programming is significant.

Levels of Interaction

Despite the numerous barriers to working together, it is possible to identify ways to join efforts in the best interest of the elderly. Often when beginning to work together, the participants feel that success must be measured by developing a complex network of services. When this does not occur, they may feel that they have failed. This is generally not the case. There are many ways that churches and synagogues can work together with other community agencies. Even small changes are important in improving services for older people. As shown in Chart 9-1, we have identified five levels of interaction, all of which can benefit service providers and the elderly.

Communication is the simplest form of interaction, encompassing the sharing of information or ideas and including consultation that can take a variety of forms, such as giving advice or technical assistance. The next level of interaction, cooperation, is in evidence when two or more separate organizations work together to achieve a common goal but implement their programs independently. This is most beneficial when church or synagogue develops a program that is needed by the community that does not duplicate an existing program. Coordination occurs when planning and implementation occur together. Collaboration, in turn, is the sharing of resources and is present when two distinct organizations join together to provide a single program. The highest level of interaction is confederation, which refers to the merging of organizations to provide a program in which there is a merging of separate identities. This type of interaction is unlikely to occur between churches and social service agencies but has occurred among sectarian service agencies, as evidenced in communitywide Jewish Federations, Catholic Charities, and Lutheran Social Services.

Chart 9–1
Five Levels of Interaction Leading to Improved Programming

Level of Interaction	Type of Interaction
1. Communication	Verbal, written, or other forms of communication limited to sharing information or ideas between organizations. Includes consultation.
2. Cooperation	Two or more separate organizations plan and implement independent programs, but all work toward similar, nonconflicting goals. The organizations share information but act on it independently. Organizations advertise for each other and try to avoid unnecessary duplication of services.
3. Coordination	Two or more separate organizations work together to plan programs and ensure that they interact smoothly and avoid conflict, waste, and unnecessary duplicaiton of services. Organizations share information, advertise for each other, and make referrals to each other.
4. Collaboration	Two or more separate organizations join together to provide a single program or service. Each organization maintains its own identity but resources are jointly shared.
5. Confederation	Two or more organizations merge to provide programs or services. None of the participating organizations maintains a separate identity or separate resources.

An understanding of these levels can be helpful to the individual church or synagogue. Any kind of activity between organizations must begin with communication. Through communication, particularly in face-to-face interaction, an understanding and perspective of the other person's concerns and preoccupations can be achieved. Without an appreciation for the other person, trust can not be developed, and it is through knowledge and trust that true working together progresses. As was evident in the Steinitz study, busy clergy and busy social workers may not be aware of each other. Lacking knowlege, they may assume antipathies that really are not there or, if they are present, can be resolved sufficiently through communication so that cooperation and coordination can commence. Thus, if communication is successful, referrals back and forth will be initiated, followed by programmatic initiatives between one church and other, between one synagogue and another, and among churches, synagogues, and social agencies.

Application of the levels of interaction begins with some form of communication. This means that clergy and other concerned individuals from churches and synagogues need to establish communication with local social service agencies. It may be helpful to begin by discussing the types of programs and services that are available within the churches and synagogues and the social service agencies. Once communication is established, the various religious organizations and social service agencies can begin to work toward other avenues of cooperation. This may mean working together on behalf of individuals in the congregation or community, or it may mean the development of mutual programmatic efforts to solve local needs.

Working Together on Behalf of Individuals

One of the most obvious ways that churches and synagogues can work together is on behalf of particular individuals in their congregations and communities. Working with the local agency does not mean giving up all concern or contact with the individual. Rather, working together means that an ongoing contact is made that will benefit the individual in need. This can be done in several ways, through consultation, referral, conferences, and joint planning.

Consultation

When families seek out their minister for advice about an elderly family member in need of nursing home care, the minister may be very helpful in assisting the family to sort out the emotional issues related to placement. But, when they ask about which nursing homes they should consider, the minister may wish to call upon a social worker from a local hospital discharge planning department for consultation on the appropriate nursing homes to investigate. Through consultation, the minister gains needed information but maintains direct contact with his parishioner. When primary responsibility for working with the individual needs to be retained, consultation is the appropriate approach for working with others.

Referral

Referrals are useful when the church or synagogue is unable to provide the services needed by an individual member of the congregation (for a useful discussion of referrals in pastoral counseling, see Oglesby, 1978). Individual clergy, churches or synagogues cannot be expected to provide for every possible human need. When a request is made for a service that cannot be provided by the church or synagogue, it is time to make a referral.

One problem that clergy and lay persons encounter in making referrals is that the individual who obviously needs help may be unwilling to accept assistance from others. Clergy usually are acquainted with members of their congregation well enough to know such things as who consumes too much alcohol or who is having marital difficulties. However, just because someone is in need does not necessarily mean that someone is willing to seek or accept outside help. Some alcoholics are willing to discuss their problem with their pastor but not willing to go to an alcohol rehabilitation center. When this type of situation is encountered, the responsibility of clergy and concerned lay people is to assist the person in seeing a need for help. Preparation for professional counseling or medical assistance can be a difficult task, but members of the church or synagogue family can be supportive until such time that the individual is ready to seek professional assistance.

Another challenge is learning to make appropriate referrals. In two communities we studied, clergy from denominations that have their own social service agencies (Lutherans, Catholics, and Jews) made referrals only to their church- or synagogue-sponsored agency. The priest referred anyone with a problem to Catholic Charities, the rabbi to the Jewish Federation, and the Lutheran minister to Lutheran Social Services. This was appropriate when the agency receiving the referral could provide the needed service. However, in many cases the person in need was requesting services such as transportation or meals which were not available from the sectarian agencies. These services were, however, readily available from the local senior center. Thus, the congregants were being sent many miles away to talk to someone at the denominational agency who then referred them back to a secular agency that was only a short walking distance from their homes. Although it is important to support denominational agencies, it is necessary to understand what they do and do not provide before making the referral. A telephone call prior to making a referral may save congregants hours of time and frustration.

Conferences

Once the referral is made, it is useful to keep in touch with the agency to follow the progress of the client. One instance in which this is particularly important is when the person is in a mental health facility. The person with the psychiatric problem may be in a hospital, but the family still attends church or synagogue. At these and other times, clergy should consider going with appropriate consent to the mental health center for a conference with staff. The clergy can be advised in the conference as to the progress of the patient and, in turn, can advise the staff about the concerns of the family, as well as the supports available from the church or synagogue.

Joint Planning

As clergy and social service agency personnel become better acquainted, they may wish to begin to do joint planning for the needs of persons about whom they are concerned. Often the senior who has recently returned home from the hospital will have a visiting nurse and possibly a social worker coming to the home to assist with his or her needs. In these cases, the clergy or lay person also may be visiting the individual. A meeting among the various visitors could be useful in coordinating the visits and in assisting the senior in planning for the future. For example, Mrs. Smith may have a nurse, a nurse's aid, a social worker, and someone from the local church visiting her. If the visitors do not know about each other or are unwilling to coordinate their visits, Mrs. Smith may find that everyone comes to see her on Tuesday, Wednesday, and Thursday, and no one stops by from Friday to Monday. On the other hand, if the visitors do joint planning, either by telephone or in a conference-style meeting, they can space their visits enough to cover most or all of the days of the week.

Working together on behalf of individuals is generally a matter of establishing communication with people from churches, synagogues, and social service agencies. It means gaining enough familiarity to be able to send the right people to the right agency. It also means working together on behalf of the people in need. Without this communication, the person with the need may not receive help. If they do receive help, there may be duplication of efforts, and, in some cases, the various concerned people may be working against each other.

Working Together as Organizations

There are many ways that organizations can work together. They cannot do so, however, unless there is a shared agenda. The elderly are not, for example, always a primary concern. In poor communities, general survival needs may be more important than the problems of any specific age group. For those who agree to focus on problems of the elderly, in turn, there may not be agreement concerning their greatest need. Some may perceive health care to be the biggest problem; others, crime against the elderly. If there is a failure to agree on the priority of needs, there may not be any ongoing contact between organizations. Hindering the development of group cohesion may also be a "hidden agenda," as occurs when the convener calls a meeting to share concerns but really wants the others to provide buses for their congregants or clients.

To start the process, someone must spend the time bringing the group together. As we all know, it takes time and effort to gather together a group of clergy and social service personnel for cooperative planning. Particularly in communities where this type of joint planning has not taken place in the past, people need time to get to know one another and learn how to work together. Once a group is brought together, there need to be some types of follow through activities. The group needs to be able to do something more than simply meet, something like holding a joint workshop or addressing the particular needs of an individual older person. Everything, from calling the next meeting to carrying out the tasks of the group, will need to happen, or the group will soon die from lack of support. Initial efforts to bring groups together can be done in several different ways. Meetings, workshops, and surveys are some of the more successful approaches.

Meetings

The easiest way to bring persons together is simply to invite them to a meeting. But, unless meetings are carefully planned, few may attend. Paritipcants must understand why they are being brought together and what is hoped to be accomplished. Attendance may be high in smaller communities or when those invited know each other but certainly can be disappointing in larger communities and areas where people do not have previous knowledge of each other. Still, if the potential benefits are clear, there is reason to be optimistic.

Workshops

A workshop is a sensible approach when there is an apparent interest in a particular issue or concern. A workshop on the homebound elderly, for example, should appeal to these people who are currently visiting seniors. Workshops can provide an informal atmosphere for various people to get together to discuss the issues at hand. By providing written educational material, the host group supports those in attendance by giving them information that they do not already have. Planners of workshops must consider further phases and plan for them. Names of those in attendance should be gathered. Also, a short written survey evaluating the workshop should include a checklist of further activities for attendees to check for participation.

Surveys

Another way to bring people together is to share concerns revealed by a survey of potential members of the group. If each person has an opportunity to voice concerns, it is likely that he or she will be interested in the responses of others. Additionally, the initiating organization or group will better understand what the concerns are of each of the churches, synagogues, and agencies in the community. A host agency may believe that homebound seniors are not receiving the kinds of services that they need but may not be sure that others perceive the situation in the same way. Although a survey may be time consuming, if done well, it can produce a great deal of information about the types of needs and concerns perceived by professionals in the community. If the survey is done face-to-face, it facilitates further contact because of familiarity. At least one person in the group may know everyone at the meeting.

Umbrella Agencies

If community churches, synagogues, and social service agencies have achieved the first four levels of interaction found in Chart 9–1, it may be possible to reach confederation by developing an umbrella agency that can bring together the various groups, clubs, programs and services under one administration. This would reduce the amount of duplication of administrative services needed for each and provide a stronger, more highly coordinated base to address the holistic needs of the elderly. While few community coordinating projects ultimately develop into an umbrella agency, this may not be an unrealistic goal in some communities.

Summary

Working together is not easily accomplished, yet it is an important goal. Since 1980, the potential for working together has been explored by an increasing number of groups. For example, "recognition of the highly personalized nature of the volunteer care given to fellow church members has led the Robert Wood Johnson Foundation to fund interfaith coalitions to recruit, train, and supervise volunteers to provide home care to the frail elderly." Older persons are indeed a resource (see, for example, Tobin,

1985). Through knowledge and interaction, much can be initiated and, hopefully, much accomlished. In the next chapter a more ambitious beginning is discussed, that is, a model for gaining cooperation.

Chapter Ten

A Model for Increasing Interaction among Churches, Synagogues, and Social Service Agencies

T he central focus of our project has been on increasing interaction among churches and synagogues and local social service agencies. We reasoned that, even if only minimal levels of interactions were improved, the elderly could benefit. Sharing of information, for example, could lead to more appropriate referrals by churches and synagogues to social service agencies and vice versa. Social service agencies could also provide technical assistance on program development when needed by churches and synagogues. Moreover, a modest amount of communication could then lead to greater cooperation between groups and possibly even to coordination of programs. (See Chart 9-1 for a definition of the five levels of interaction.) Given the obstacles involved in working together and the constraints on both kinds of groups, a modest beginning is often necessary. However, if the importance of helping the elderly in the community is shared by people of goodwill, these modest beginnings can eventually lead to the development of more meaningful programs for the elderly.

The Community Advocacy Model

In an effort to facilitate the interaction among churches, synagogues, and social service agencies, we (Ellor, Anderson-Ray and Tobin, 1983; Tobin and Ellor, 1983) developed a flexible, three-phased model, referred to as the Community Advocacy Model. Variations on the model were tested in six diverse communities. The primary goals of this model were twofold: (1) to enhance the role of the church and synagogue in providing for the elderly, and (2) to encourage interaction between religious congregations and social service agencies on behalf of older people.

The first of the three phases focused on the development of a working relationship with a "lead agency" in each community. This lead agency served as a point of entry and base of operations in the community. In an effort to facilitate the development of the relationship with the lead agency and to support the efforts of the project, a project assistant was assigned to the lead agency. The role of this staff member was to act both as an advocate for the elderly and as a "neutral" person who could mediate between social service agencies and churches or synagogues by making contacts, suggesting ideas, and moderating disputes. Another important task during phase one was to develop better understanding of the community by making informal contacts and working with community leaders to establish strategies for future work.

The second phase started with a systematic survey of clergy in the community, using a standardized questionnaire. The interview questionnaire was designed to provide a profile of needs of the elderly as perceived by the clergy. Included in the survey were queries on current church- and synagogue-sponsored program (using the inventory of programs on Table 5–1), on gaps in services for the elderly, on ways to enable the elderly to participate in programs and help others, on barriers to collaborating, and on willingness to participate with other clergy and service personnel in developing services for the elderly. In addition to gathering useful information, the survey was designed to sensitize clergy to the needs of the elderly and to prompt consideration of alternative strategies for addressing those needs. In two communities, social service personnel were also interviewed. Further, we attempted to survey a small sample of elderly persons in each community.

With the completion of the surveys, the third phase began. Survey results were compiled and presented at a meeting of clergy and social service agency representatives. After discussing the findings, plans for future activities were considered. In some cases, clergy asked for assistance with individual efforts in their churches, while others expressed interest in planning joint activities or programs among churches, synagogues, and social service agencies. After this point, community leaders were expected to take the primary initiative in planning and developing programs, but the project staff remained available to provide consultation regarding program development and to support collaborative efforts.

The Six Communities

The six communities which were part of our study varied greatly from one another, as did the nature of the lead agencies. Some of the basic characteristics of these communities are summarized on Table 10-1.

Our first community, Ridgeview, was a blue-collar suburb with a relatively high percentage of elderly (18.7%). The community was almost totally white and predominantly Catholic. The Ridgeview Council on Aging sponsored an areawide Senior Center and an Information and Referral Center to the community. In addition, this agency was involved in coordinating services for the elderly. The Ridgeview Council on Aging also served as our lead agency in this community.

Walnut Heights, our second community, was a more affluent, white-collar suburb. While it was also predominantly Catholic, it contained several smaller, mainline Protestant churches. With only 4.4 percent of the population being

Chart 10–1
Selected Characteristics of Communities in Our Study

Characteristics[1]	Ridgeview	Walnut Heights	Parkside	Edgewood	Elmtown	Lakeside
Population	108,081	13,625	31,935	96,428	54,887	39,786
Racial Composition[2]	93.0% White .1% Black 5.9% Hispanic 1.0% Other	92.5% White 3.0% Black 1.4% Hispanic 3.1% Other	.3% White 99.0% Black .6% Hispanic .1% Other	44% White 9% Black 57% Hispanic 0% Other	83.5% White 10.8% Black 2.5% Hispanic 3.3% Other	27.9% White 29.7% Black 42.3% Hispanic .1% Other
Median Income for Households	$17,278	$26,123	n.a.	n.a.	$20,601	$17,180
Percent of Persons in Poverty	7.4%	2.8%	n.a.	n.a.	5.1%	16.8%
Percent of Population 65 years or older	18.7%	4.4%	n.a.	n.a.	14.2%	10.5%
Approximate Number of Churches, Synagogues, and Other Religious Institutions	51	7	40	81	55	45
Religious Affiliation	Predominantly Roman Catholic, with fewer mainline Protestants	Predominantly Roman Catholic, with fewer mainline Protestants	Mixed	Predominantly Roman Catholic. Many Fundamentalist and a few non-Christian Groups. Few mainline Protestants.	Predominantly Roman Catholic. Many mainline Protestants and two Synagogues, several non-Christian Groups.	Predominantly Roman Catholic. Many Fundamentalist and Protestant Churches. One Synagogue

Chart 10–1 (continued)
Selected Characteristics of Communities in Our Study

Approximate number of Social Service Agencies	n.a.	n.a.	33	38	25
Lead Agency	Ridgeview Council on Aging	Walnut Heights Park District	People's Church	None	First Church

Areawide Community Mental Health Center

[1] Population, racial composition, income, poverty, and age statistics based on 1980 U.S. Census data.

[2] Persons of Spanish descent may belong to either white or black racial groups.

elderly, there had been relatively little interest in serving this age group. The Park District was the only agency in this small community with a program for the elderly. Thus, it became the lead agency for this community.

Our third community, Parkside, was a poor inner-city community. The majority of the residents were black. Unemployment was extremely high. There was a diversity of churches in the community, including many storefront churches and one well-established church (People's Church) that was built when the neighborhood was relatively affluent. Although many parishioners of People's Church did not live in the neighborhood, the church was very committed to helping the community. The importance of this church's leadership, coupled with the dearth of social service agencies located in the community, led us to use People's Church as our lead agency.

The fourth community, Edgewood, was also a poor, inner-city community. Long serving as a "port of entry" to new racial and ethnic groups, this community had become more than half Hispanic. However, many of the elderly were Eastern Europeans who immigrated to the United States at the turn of the century. The elderly now comprised about 8 percent of the population. Some of these seniors still did not speak English. A predominantly Catholic community, there were many social service agencies but few programs designed explicitly for the elderly. Because of the rigid structure of the service system in this community, we were unable to locate a lead agency willing to work toward the goals of developing services for the elderly and enhancing interaction between community groups.

The fifth community, Elmtown, was an upper middle-class suburb community with a relatively high percentage of elderly (14.2 percent). Once again, this suburb was predominantly white, although it was slowly becoming more racially integrated. This was a "service rich" community, with many agencies serving the elderly. First Church, a large mainline Protestant church, was our lead agency.

The sixth and final community, Lakeside, was located in a heavily industrial area. Hispanics and blacks outnumbered the white population in this community. While predominantly Catholic, there were many fundamentalist Protestant churches, a few mainline Protestant churches, and one synagogue serving this community. Although only about 10 percent of the population was elderly, there were numerous agencies to serve them. Our lead agency was the areawide Community Mental Health Center (CMHC).

The Community Advocacy Model

General Findings

We were continually impressed with the level of concern for the elderly expressed by clergy and social service personnel. Both groups were able to identify the critical needs of the elderly in their communities. In poor communities, the needs identified were associated with issues of survival that transcended age per se. In the other communities, the need for specialized programs for the elderly was identified. Further, when needs such as transportation or housing for the elderly were identified, those concerns were generally mentioned by both clergy and social service agency personnel, although they may have been ranked in slightly different order. Other needs commonly recognized among respondents in both groups were the elderly's need for social activities, health and medical services, and support services which would allow older people to live independently in their own homes.

While most clergy were very sensitive to the needs of older people, the diversity among churches in their support of social service programs was striking. At one extreme, a large church was identified which had fifty-two staff members and operated essentially as a multipurpose social service agency. It provided services ranging from senior citizens' housing to social and recreational activities. At the opposite extreme was a small, fundamentalist church staffed by a single pastor who refused to sponsor activities that were not directly related to the salvation of souls. Clergy identified a number of barriers which prohibited the development of additional programs for the elderly. Lack of lay leadership was the most frequently mentioned barrier to program development, with lack of resources and demands on the busy schedules of clergy also frequently mentioned in most communities.

Regarding collaboration, we found scattered programs supported by ecumenical groups of churches or jointly sponsored by churches and social service agencies. The most commonly shared programs among churches were ecumenically supported worship services and efforts to provide food to the needy, particularly at holidays. In several communities, however, programs were identified which were provided through joint efforts of churches and social service agencies. These included a hospital-based, home-delivered meals program which relied on church volunteers to deliver meals, as well as several visitation programs and a screening service for a blood bank which were supported by churches. While there was not extensive interaction among churches, synagogues, and social service agencies in these communities, some clergy expressed interest in meetings with social service agencies to exchange information about services, while nearly all indicated interest in attending workshops on the topics of aging or working with the elderly.

Effects of the Community Advocacy Model

Building on interests expressed through the interview process, efforts were made in each community to assist individual churches and synagogues in developing programs for the elderly and to encourage interaction among churches, synagogues, and social service agencies. Observable outcomes varied widely, from having virtually no success to establishing groups interested in sponsoring collaborative programs.

We were least successful in Edgewood, the predominantly Hispanic, inner-city neighborhood where we were not even able to establish a lead agency willing to sponsor our project. Although we approached both a leading community action agency and a well-established Catholic church, neither would take on the project. A barrier to becoming established in this community was our research orientation, as well as our tie to a major university. With time, however, we also learned there were deep divisions in the community. While there was a modicum of interaction between churches and social service agencies, it became clear that there were rigid and narrowly defined patterns of interaction. Shifting these patterns would have been a formidable task which would likely have taken years to accomplish. We found that there were already several umbrella groups working toward the goal of increasing collaboration, but, unfortunately, none was assessed to be compatible with our timetable or defined intervention strategy. Given these problems, the decision was made to invest our energies in other communities.

Our strategy for change was also not well received in the inner-city poor black community, Parkside. It was, therefore, altered in response to the unique characteristics of this community. Essentially, we dropped the formal interview process and used more informal contacts to meet clergy and collect information. Since survival needs for residents of all ages were great, our narrow focus on the needs of the elderly was not seen as consistent with the priorities in the community. Feeling overwhelmed by the urgency of survival needs for the entire community, key clergy suggested that community redevelopment, rather than enhancing services to the elderly, was the primary concern. Thus, our task shifted to supporting the lead agency in bringing together the clergy council to act on redevelopment efforts, as well as to establish a senior citizens' social action group developed to address issues, including crime. We worked with the clergy council to generate a proposal to hire a community redevelopment specialist who could obtain needed funds to support redevelopment efforts.

In the more affluent suburb, Walnut Heights, results were mixed. While clergy agreed to be interviewed, they were unwilling to join together in an ecumenical effort to improve services for the elderly. Refusal of the Catholic church

to participate in efforts, coupled with competition for survival among the small Protestant churches, prevented this
type of interaction. Personality conflicts among professionals
in this community were also a problem. Subsequent efforts
with one of the Protestant churches, however, led to spon-
sorship of a series of classes on aging. Open to anyone in the
community, the course attracted participants from several
churches and spurred interest in developing an outreach program for the elderly living in a nearby senior citizen's housing unit.

In Elmtown, the other relatively affluent white-color
suburb, results were once again mixed. Given the academic
orientation of this community, our intervention strategy was
very well received. Clergy, service personnel, and elderly
persons were interviewed. Attendance was high at the community meeting to discuss our findings. Significantly,
members of the local welfare council and senior coordinating
council attended the meeting. Several specific projects were
proposed which involved cooperative efforts between clergy
and social service personnel. One was a specific request
from a home-health agency staff member for support from
clergy in providing counseling and pastoral care services to
her homebound patients. One pastor responded positively to
this idea, and a discussion ensued about developing a referral system whereby clergy would be available to visit these
homebound patients. After the pastor responded positively
to this idea, a discussion ensued about developing a referral
system whereby clergy would be available to visit these
homebound patients.

A second concern which was raised at this meeting was
the need for a comprehensive directory of services that
would be available to churches and social service agencies.
During this discussion the program director of a church-
sponsored social services program mentioned that a directory had been compiled by an ecumenical volunteer
organization. Unfortunately, they did not have the needed
assistance to duplicate, collate, and distribute the directory.
The program director then expressed a willingness to share

the directory with the group but requested assistance in compiling and distributing the directory. Several people at the meeting responded to this request.

Our efforts were most successful in the two blue-collar communities of Ridgeview and Lakeside. In Ridgeview, our methodology was well received. It led to obtaining contacts which resulted in both increased programming for the elderly in three local churches and collaborative efforts between the lead agency and several churches. Specifically, a senior center and two programs for the homebound were initiated after consultation with the project staff. In addition, a series of workshops led by local clergy was provided by the lead agency for staff, and the number of requests for technical assistance in program development received by the lead agency from local churches also increased.

In the final community, Laketown, we were very successful. This was due largely to the commitment by the lead agency, the Community Mental Health Center (CMHC), to developing a positive rapport with clergy and supporting communitywide efforts to improve services for the elderly. We were able to interview about half the clergy in the community, most of whom were affiliated with Roman Catholic, Orthodox, and mainline Protestant churches. We had a great deal of difficulty, however, contacting and interviewing clergy from the more fundamentalist and storefront churches. Personnel from all twelve of the identified social service agencies which served the elderly were interviewed.

As we have reported (Tobin, et al., 1985), the CMHC serves a large industrial area of 40,000, half of whom are nonwhite. One of five distinctly different communities served by the CMHC was selected, an urbanized heterogeneous low-income area (median per capita income of $6,499). Although the CMHC provides inpatient and many outpatient services, it has no specific program for the elderly. The director expressed interest in developing a working relationship with the churches in his service area, particularly regarding the elderly, and our Community Advocacy Project was linked primarily to the Consultation and Education (C&E) Department.

The surveys, particularly of CMHC personnel, helped to increase awareness of issues and also developed curiosity about how their responses compared to others. The surveys, however, also revealed, among other findings, that referrals were uncommon and that there were many obstacles to collaboration, including the clergy's perception that CMHC personnel did not appreciate the role of religion in the lives of their clients and CMHC personnel's perceptions that clergy proselytize and are not trained to provide counseling.

Yet, a group of CMHC personnel, clergy, and staff from social service agencies who were in the surveys were willing to meet to discuss collaboration. The tone of the initial breakfast meeting was informal, and the discussion was lively. A number of ideas were suggested: such as a joint effort to provide preretirement and postretirement training for seniors, to develop life enrichment groups for seniors, to develop a comprehensive directory listing programs provided by social service agencies and churches, to invite clergy to participate in monthly family committee meetings, to discuss clergy visiting the CMHC jointly planned workshops, and to form a short-term task force to plan collaborative activities in the community.

A report containing the findings from the surveys was then mailed to all of the clergy and service providers who were not able to attend the commuinity meeting. In the follow-up activities, CMHC exhibited willingness to carry through specific responsibilities, such as using project staff as consultants, working with a local senior center, developing the comprehensive directory, and beginning to develop a training program to help staff learn more about working with local clergy, and the CMHC also committed itself to work toward establishing new policies and procedures for working with clergy.

A task force composed of CMHC personnel, local clergy, and mental health professionals representing other community agencies then started meeting monthly to discuss a variety of theological and psycholosocial issues as they related to counseling clients or parishioners. Discussions were lively and informative, focusing on the topic selected by the committee. Such topics as suffering, divorce, love and marriage, and helping people help themselves were included. Some discussion sessions opened with case presentations by either a therapist or clergyperson, and other sessions began with less formality. The group expressed ideas, perceptions, commonalities, and differences during six monthly meetings.

At the spring meeting, eight clergy and six mental health professionals evaluated their progress. The consensus was to discontinue the meetings during the summer months and to reconvene in the fall with a more structured agenda. One member suggested utilizing the expertise of individual committee members to learn from one another. Several training topics were suggested for the fall, including stress, how sacred writings can be used in counseling, therapy with the oppressed, black theology and pastoral counseling, grief and loss, counseling the elderly, the hospice movement, and abused older adults. Comments were very favorable, and additional types of coordinated efforts were mentioned, such as having therapists and clergy co-lead groups and having clergy refer their parisioners to groups offered at the CMHC. Clearly, CMHC personnel and clergy became aware of shared issues and showed an openness toward working together. Of significance is that during the one and one-half years of the project, by the end of the summer, referrals of elderly to the CMHC increased from two to seventeen.

The success we had is apparently unique. Obviously, there is an interest in the potential of this kind of collaboration between CMHCs and religious institutions (see, for example, Pargament, 1982). Yet, the published reports focus on potential rather than actual successes (see, for example, Pratt and Kethley, 1980, and Wilson and Simson, 1980).

Summary of the Results

During the three-year time span of our project, we learned a great deal from both the successes and failures of our model. We learned that there is relatively little interaction among churches, synagogues, and social service agencies beyond a few traditional church-sponsored activities. Further, interest in developing collaborative efforts varies tremendously.

A variety of factors were found which inhibit or otherwise limit the extent to which churches, synagogues, and social service agencies are willing to interact. Lack of knowledge about the types of programs and services that each group has to offer is one type of problem. Another is unfounded stereotypes and misconceptions of each other which can present barriers as attempts are made to foster more interaction. Additionally, clergy and social service personnel frequently have very similar motives, but often they use a different language to express themselves, as well as different strategies for taking action. In order to encourage collaboration, each group needs to understand the strategies and language of the other. When efforts can be made to establish personal contacts between these groups, and a common language defined for communicating with each other, it is possible to move toward collaboration. When this cannot be done, collaboration is not possible.

We also learned that a common goal is essential to encouraging collaboration. In our experience, we found that not all communities are equally willing to work toward developing programs specifically for the elderly. This was particularly apparent in the more impoverished community in which the survival needs of all community residents were equally willing to work toward developing programs specifically for the elderly. This was particularly apparent in the more impoverished community in which the survival needs of all community residents were great. In these cases, we found it more useful to begin with the greatest needs identified by the community leaders. In the case of Parkside, this meant beginning with broad community redevelopment goals. While not designed specifically for the elderly, this type of program clearly held the potential for improving the community for all residents, including older people.

Finally, we learned that some groups are simply unwilling or unable to participate in collaborative efforts. A variety of factors will influence the extent to which churches and synagogues become involved in working collaboratively to provide services to the elderly. The church's or synagogue's understanding of itself as an institution is of critical importance. Most churches and synagogues perceive themselves primarily as religious institutions. As they move into developing social service programs, theological consistency is thus very important in shaping programming. To become involved in collaborative efforts, the church or synagogue must be willing to support the concept of social ministry. Further, some theologies severely limit willingness to participate in ecumenical activities or other types of combined programming efforts with community groups. Another important consideration is the availability of resources to develop new programs. Financial resources are obviously important, but we also learned that lay leadership and demands on the clergy's time can limit program development. It is evident, when the various problems and barriers to programming are made clear, that social service agencies, churches, and synagogues struggle with very similar types of problems.

Looking at our successes, we learned that it is essential to have an established, stable individual or a strong group based in the community to provide leadership for collaborative efforts. A group of committed community leaders is often best, since losing one or two persons will probably not cause the project to lose all of its momentum. Further, by working with a group which includes a variety of clergy and social service personnel, the project will more likely be accepted by many different groups in the community.

Commitment to working with others and time to slowly build solid relationships within the community are also essential to success. Developing good programs can often take years of consistent applied effort. This process generally begins by developing mutual understanding and trust among community groups, including the churches, synagogues, and social service agencies. Particularly where interaction has been absent, it will take time to begin new efforts.

Flexibility and the willingness to creatively adjust strategies for change in each unique community are also important keys to success. The Community Advocacy Model was developed with the basic assumption that churches and synagogues can benefit from interaction with one another and with social service agencies. Yet, as we applied the model in our diverse communities, it became clear that expected goals and outcomes must be adjusted to the needs and interests of each community. Because no two communities are exactly alike, adjustments are necessary to fit the leadership style, community characteristics, and needs of the elderly in that particular locality.

While we encountered many obstacles to increasing collaborative activities, it is our belief that churches and synagogues can work singly or collectively with community agencies to improve services to the elderly. This process clearly takes time commitment, but the potential benefit to older people suggests that it is worth the effort.

Epilogue

We have described many ways that churches and synagogues can serve the elderly within the community service system. Not only can programs be developed within the walls of church and synagogue, but clergy and laity can move outward to serve the homebound and those in nursing homes, as well as ministering to the dying and their families. In these several efforts, important allies are social service agencies. Indeed, by understanding and working with social service agencies, the needs of the elderly can be better met in a manner which is both holistic and honors the uniqueness of each individual.

During the past three years in which we have worked actively with clergy and social service personnel, we have found an enormous commitment to serving the elderly. Yet, there are barriers to translating this commitment into action. Taking on an additional agenda and an additional challenge, in an already overburdened schedule, never can be taken lightly, but, if ways to meet the new challenge are understood, the new task need not be so difficult. Our purpose has been to provide a knowledge base, as well as specific guidelines, so that the process of program development for the elderly can be accomplished.

If new initiatives are indeed forthcoming after the reading of our text, we will have achieved our goal. Still, we are not naive. It is only through commitment, knowledge, and hard work that the best of thoughts are translated into deeds. Ours have been the easier task, as we have discussed some principles and some action steps. But the task of others is more difficult. It is to work collaboratively to develop programs that meet the needs of elderly individuals.

References

Atchley, R.C. (1976). *The Sociology of Retirement*. New York: Schenkman Publishing Co.

Beattie, W.M. (1963). A research project in church services to the aging. *Review of Religious Research*, 4, 108–116.

Blazer, D., and Palmore, E. (1976). Religion and in a longitudinal panel. *The Gerontologist*, 16, 82–84.

Breckenridge, E, Lave, H, Little, M.H., and Burgess, E.W. (1952). *Community Services for Older People*. Chicago: Wilcox and Follet.

Butler, R. (1963). The life review: An interpretation of reminiscence in aged. *Psychiatry*, 26, 65–76.

Cath, S.H. (1965). Some dynamics of middle and later years: A study of depletion and restitution. In M. Berezin and S. Cath (Eds.), *Geriatric Psychiatry: Grief, Loss and Emotional Disorders in the Aging Process*. New York: International Universities Press, Inc.

Clements, W.M. (1981). *Ministry with the Aging*. New York: Harper and Row.

Clingan, D.F. (1980). *Aging Persons in the Community of Faith*. New revised edition. St. Louis, Missouri: Christian Board of Publication.

177

Cohler, B.J. (1982). Adult developmental psychology and reconstruction in psychoanalysis, S.I. Greenspan and G.H. Pollock (Eds.), *The Course of Life*. Washington, D.C.: National Institute of Mental Health.

Comptroller General of the United States (1977). *Report to Congress: The Well-Being of Older People in Cleveland, Ohio*. Washington, D.C.: U.S. General Accounting Office.

Cook, T.C. Jr. (1976). *The Religious Sector Explores its Mission in Aging*. Athens, Georgia: National Interfaith Coalition on Aging.

Davidson, G.W. (1975). *Living with Dying*. Minneapolis, Minn: Augsberg Publishing House.

Diggory, J., and Rothman D.Z. (1961). Values destroyed by death. *Journal of Abnormal and Social Psychology, 30,* 11–17.

Ellor, J.W. (1983). Bridging churches and social service agencies. *Social Work and Christianity, 10,* 1–29.

Ellor, J.W., and Tobin, S.S. (1985). Beyond visitation: ministries to the homebound elderly. *Journal of Pastoral Counseling, 39,* 12–21.

Erikson, E.H. (1950). *Childhood and Society*. New York: W.W. Norton.

Erickson, E.H. (1959). Identity and the life cycle. *Psychological Issues* Monograph I. New York: International Universities Press.

Field, M. (1972). *The Aged, the Family, and the Community*, New York: Columbia University Press.

Froland, C., Pancoast, D.L., Chapman, N.J., and Kimboko, P.J. (1981). *Helping Networks and Human Services*. Beverly Hills, California: Sage Publications.

Gendel, M.H., and Reiser, D.E. (1981). Institutional countertransference. *American Journal of Psychiatry, 138,* 508–511.

Golant, S.M. (1984). *A Place to Grow Old: The Mourning of Environment in Old Age*. New York: Columbia University Press.

Goldfarb, A.I. (1959). Minor maladjustments in the aged. In S. Arieti (Ed.) *American Handbook of Psychiatry* Vol. I. New York: Basic Books.

Gorney, J. (1968). *Experiencing and age patterns of reminiscence among the elderly*. Unpublished doctoral dissertation. University of Chicago, Chicago, Illinois.

Gray, R., and Moberg, D.O. (1977). *The Church and the Older Person*. Grand Rapids, Michigan: Erdman's.

Grunes, J.M. (1981). Reminiscences, regression, and empathy - a psychotherapeutic approach to the impaired elderly. In S.I. Greenspan and G.H. Pollock (Eds.), *The Course of Life*, Washington D.C.: National Institute of Mental Health.

Gutmann, D. (1977) The cross-cultural perspective: Notes toward a comparative psychology of aging. In J.E. Birren and K.W. Schaie (Eds.), *Handbook of the Psychology of Aging*. New York: Van Nostrand Reinhold Company.

Harris, L. et al (1975). *The Myth and Reality of Aging in America.*. Washington, D.C.: National Council on the Aging.

Heisel, M.A., and Faulkner, A.O. (1982). Religiosity in an older Black polpulation. *The Gerontologist, 22*, 354–358.

Hiltner, S. (1975). *Toward a Theology of Aging*. New York: Human Sciences Press.

Hunsberger, B. (1985). Religion, age, life satisfaction and perceived sources of religiousness: A study of older persons. *Journal of Gerontology, 40*, 615–620.

Hutchenson, R.G., Jr. (1979). *Wheel Within a Wheel*. Atlanta, Georgia: Knox Press.

Huyck, M., and Hoyer, W. (1982). *Adult Development and Aging*. Belmont, California: Wadsworth.

Kalish, R.A., and Reynolds, D.K. (1976). *Death and Ethnicity: A Psycho-cultural Study*. Los Angeles: Ethel Percy Andrews Gerontology Center, University of Southern California.

Kubler-Ross, E. (1969). *On Death and Dying*. New York: MacMillian.

Kulys, R., and Tobin, S.S. (1980). Older people and their responsible others. *Social Work, 25*, 138–145.

LeFevre, C., and LeFevre, P. (1981). *Aging and the Human Spirit*. Chicago: Exploration Press.

LeFevre, P. (1984). Toward a theology of aging. *The Chicago Theology Seminal Register, 74,* 1–12.

Lieberman, M.A., and Tobin, S.S. (1983). *The Experience of Old Age: Stress, Coping, and Survival.* New York: Basic Books.

Lopata, H. (1973) *Widowhood is an American City.* Cambridge, Mass: Schenkman.

Lutheran Brotherhood (1975). *Guide for Survivors.* Minneapolis, Minn.: Lutheran Brotherhood.

Lyons, W. (1982). Coping with cognitive impairment: Some family dynamics and helping roles. *Journal of Gerontological Social Work, 4,* 3–20.

Malcolmson, J.A. (1980). *A Study for the determination of an intentional and discriminating ministry of pastoral home visitation,* Unpublished doctoral dissertation. The Eastern Baptist Theological Semrinary. Philadelphia, Pennsylvania.

Markides, K.S. (1983). Aging, religiosity, and adjustment: A longitudinal analysis, *Journal of Gerontology, 5,* 621–625.

Maves, Paul. (1960). Religion and the church. In Tibbitts, C. (Ed.) *Handbook of Social Gerontololgy.* Chicago: University of Chicago Press.

Mendelson, M.A. (1974). *Tender Loving Greed.* New York: Alfred A. Knopf.

Moss, F.E. and Halamandaris, V.J. (1977). *Too Old, Too Sick, Too Bad: Nursing Homes in America.* Germantown, Maryland: Aspen Systems Corporation.

Munnichs, J. M. (1966). *Old Age and Finitude.* New York: Karger.

Naperstek, A.M. (1978). *Clergy's role in help-seeking and receiving in urban ethnic neighborhoods.* Unpublished manuscript. University of Southern California, Washington Public Affairs, Washington, D.C.

Neugarten, B.L. (1974) Age groups in American society and the risk of the young-old. In Eis, F. (Ed.) *Political Consequences of Aging,* Philadelphia: American Academy of Political and Social Sciences.

Neugarten, B.L. (1977). Personality and aging. In J.E. Birren and K.W. Schaie (Eds.), *Handbook of the Psychology of Aging.* New York: Van Nostrand Reinhold Co., 626–649.

Neugarten, B.L. (1982). Older people: A profile. In Neugarten, B.L. (Ed). *Age or Need?* Beverly Hills, California: Sage Publications.

Oglesby, W.B. (1978). *Referral in Pastoral Counseling,* Nashville Tenn: Abingdon Press.

O'Hare, D.G. (1982). The experience of dying. In G. Lesnoff-Caravaglia (Ed.), *Aging and the Human Condition.* New York: Human Sciences Press.

Ostrovsky, R. (1985). *Renewal in a congregation: Establishing a health cabinet. Conservative Judaism, 38,* 62–70.

Palmore, E. (1980). The social factors in aging. In E. Busse and D. Blazer (Eds.) *Handbook of Geriatric Psychiatry.* New York Van Nostrand Reinhold.

Pargament, K.I. (1982). The interface among religion, religious support systems and mental health. In D. Biegal and A. Naperstek (Eds.), *Community Support Systems and Mental Health.* (New York: Springer Publishing Co.

Pinkus, L. (1976) *Death and the Family.* New York: Pantheon Books.

Pratt, C., and Kethley, A. (1980). Anticipated and actual barriers to developing mental health programs for the elderly. *Community Mental Health Journal, 16,* 205–216.

Reider, N. (1953). A type of transference to institutions. *Journal of the Hillside Hospital, 2,* 23–29.

Revere, V., and Tobin, S.S. (1980–1981). Myth and reality: the older person's relationship to his past. *International Journal of Aging and Human Development, 12,* 15–26.

Riley, M.W., and Foner, A. (1968). *Aging and Society.* New York: Russell Sage Foundation.

Robb, T.B. (1981). Ministry with 'grays'. *Presbyterian Survey, 21,* 40–41.

Robinson, P. Coberly, S. and PaulC. (1985). Work and retirement. In R.H. Birnstock and E. Shanas (Ed.), *Handbook of Aging and the Social Sciences.* New York: Van Nostrand Reinhold Co.

Rosner, A. (1968). Stress and the maintenance of self-concept in the aged. Unpublished doctoral dissertation. University of Chicago, Chicago, Illinois.

Rossi, R.J., Gilmartin, K.J. and Dayton, C.W. (1982). *Agencies Working Together.* Beverly Hills, California: Sage Publications.

Safirstein, S.L. (1967). Institutional transference. *Psychiatric Quarterly, 41,* 557–566.

Saunders, C. (1969). The moment of truth: Care of the dying person. In L. Pearson (Ed.), *Death and Dying.* Cleveland: The Press of Case Western University.

Schlesenger, M.R., Tobin, S.S., and Kulyn, R. (1981). The responsible child and parental well-being. *Journal of Gerontological Social Work, 3,* 3–16.

Schmitt, A. (1967). *Dialogue with Death.* Waco, Texas: Ward Incorporated.

Schneidman, E.S. (1973). *The Deaths of Man.* New York: Quadrangle Press.

Shanas, E. and Maddox, G. (1976). Aging health and the organization of health resources. In R.H. Binstock and E. Shanas (Eds.), *Handbook of Aging and the Social Sciences.* New York: Van Nostrand Reinhold Co.

Shanas, E., Townsend, P., Weddenburn, D., in Friis, H, Milhoj, P., and Stehouwer, J. (1968). *Old People in Three Industrial Societies.* New York: Athedon Press.

Snyder, R. (1981). Religious meaning in the latter third of life, *Religious Education, 76,* 534.

Steinitz, L.Y. (1980) Religiosity, well-being and Weltanshung among the Elderly. *Journal for the Scientific Study of Religion, 19,* 60–67.

Steinitz, L.Y. (1980). *The church within the network of social services to the elderly*: Case Study of Laketown. Unpublished doctoral dissertation. University of Chicago. Chicago, Illinois.

Steinitz, L.Y. (1981). The local church as support for the elderly. *Journal of Gerontological Social Work, 4,* 43–53.

Stone, H.W. and Garner, J.W. (1981). Affiliate relationship and methods of cooperation between a community mental health center and religious counseling agency. *The Journal of Pastoral Care, 36,* 246–249.

Sussman, M.B. (1985). Family life of the elderly. In R.H. Binstock and E. Shanas (Eds.), *Handbook of Aging and the Social Sciences,* New York: Van Nostrand Reinhold Co.

Thorson, J. and Cook, T.C. (1980) *Spiritual Well-Being of the Elderly.* Springfield, Illinois: Charles C. Thomas Press.

Tobin, S.S. (1966). Understanding elderly. In H.L. Jacobs and W.W. Morris (Eds.), *Nursing and Retirement Home Administration.* Ames, Iowa: Iowa State Univ. Press.

Tobin, S.S. (1972). The earliest memory as data for research in aging. In R. Kastenbaum and S. Sherwood (Eds.), *Research, Planning and Action for the Elderly: Power and Potential of Social Sciences.* New York: Behavioral Publications.

Tobin, S.S. (1985). Older Americans as a resource. In T. Tedrick (Ed.), *Aging: Issues and Policies for the 80's.* New York: Praeger Press.

Tobin, S.S., and Ellor, J.W. (1983). The church and the aging network: more interaction needed. *Generations, 8,* 26–29.

Tobin, S.S. and Lieberman, M.A. (1976). *A Last Home for the Aged: Critical Implications of Institutionalization.* San Francisco: Jossey-Bass.

Tobin, S.S., Anderson-Ray, S.M., Ellor, M.W., and Ehrenpreis, T. (1985). Enhancing CMHC and church collaboration for the elderly. *Community Mental Health Journal, 21,* 53–61.

Townsend, C. (1971). *Old Age: The Last Segregation.* New York: Grossman Publishers.

Troll, L., Miller, S.J., and Atchley, R.C. (1970). *Families in Later Life,* Belmont, California: Wadsworth.

Turner, B.F., Tobin, S.S., and Lieberman, M.A. (1972). Personality traits as predictors of institutional adaptation among the aged. *Journal of Gerontology, 27,* 61–68.

United States Senate, Special Committee on Aging (1982). *Developments in Aging: 1981,* Washington, D.C.: U.S. Government Printing Office.

184 REFERENCES

U.S. Bureau of the Census (1982) *Statistical Abstract of the United States 1982–1983*. 103rd edition. Washington, D.C.: U.S. Government Printing Office.

U.S. General Accounting Office. (1979). *Entering a Nursing Home—Costly Implications for Medicaid and the Elderly*. Washington, D.C.: U.S. General Accounting Office.

U.S. National Center for Health Statistics (1979). *The National Nursing Home Survey: 1977 Summary for the United States*. Washington, D.C.: U.S. Government Printing Office.

U.S. National Center for Health Statistics (1980).*Health, United States: 1980*. Washington, D.C.: U.S. Government Printing Office.

U.S. National Center for Health Statistics (1982). 1981 Annual Summary of Births, Deaths, Marriages and Divorces. *Monthly Vital Statistics Report*. Vol. 30. No. 13. DHHS Publication No. (PHS) 83–1120, Hyattsville, MD: Public Health Service.

Vladek, B. (1980). *Unloving Care: The Nursing Home Tragedy*. New York: Basic Books, Inc.

Van Eck, L.A. J.M. (1972). Transference to the hospital. *Psychotherapy and Psychosomatics, 20,* 135–138.

Veroff, J., Kulka, R.A., and Douvan, E. (1981). *Mental Health in America: Patterns of Help-seeking from 1957 to 1976*. New York: Basic Books.

Vincente, L., Wiley, J.A., and Carrington, R.A. (1979). The risk of institutionalization before death. *The Gerontologist, 19,* 361–367.

Vowler, R.M. (1983). Pastoral visitation re-defined. *The Clergy Journal, 59,* 18.

Weinberg, J. (1974). What do I say to my mother when I have nothing to say? *Geriatrics, 29,* 155–159.

Wilmer, H.A. (1962). Transference to a medical center. *California Medicine, 96,* 173–180.

Wilson, L., and Simson, S. (1980). Community mental health centers and the elderly: A time for expansion of planning, research and demonstration projects. *Community Mental Health Journal, 16,* 276–282.

Worley, R.C. (1978). *Dry Bones Breath!* Chicago: Center for the Study of Church Organizational Behavior.

Index of Proper Names

Atchley, R. C., 7, 64

Beattie, W. M., 144
Blazer, D., 28
Breckenridge, E., 143–44
Butler, R., 24

Clements, W. M., 16
Clingan, D. F., 16, 44
Cook, T. C., 30–32

Davidson, G. W., 121, 140
Diggory, J., 124

Ellor, J. W., 76–78, 146
Erikson, E. H., 21

Field, M., 65
Froland, C., 29

Goland, S. M., 8
Gray, R., 28
Grunes, J., 24

Harris, L., 27
Heisel, M. A., 28
Hiltner, S., 16
Hunsberger, B., 28

Hutchenson, R. G., Jr., 30
Huyck, M., 131–32

Kalish, R. A., 124
Kubler-Ross, E., 126–27

LeFevre, C., 16
LeFevre, P., 20–21
Lieberman, M. A., 4, 125–26
Lopata, H., 133

Maimonides, 16–17
Malcolmson, J. A., 23–24, 75
Markides, K. S., 28
Maves, Paul, 29
Mendelsohn, M. A., 106
Moss, F. E., 106
Munnichs, J. M., 4, 124–25

Naperstek, A. M., 22
Neugarten, B. L., 3–4, 5, 63–64

Oglesby, W. B., 151
O'Hare, D. G., 127–28
Ostrovsky, R., 16–17

Palmore, E., 27
Pargament, K. I., 171

Pinkus, L., 133–34
Pratt, C., 171

Riley, M. W., 27
Robb, T. B., 8
Robinson, P., 64
Rossi, R. J., 144

Saunders, C., 135
Schmitt, A., 140
Schneidman, E. S., 121, 127
Shanas, E., 76
Snyder, R., 21
Steinitz, L. Y., viii, 28, 30, 48,
    145–46, 150

Stone, H. W., 145
Sussman, M. B., 7

Thorson, J., 18–19
Tobin, S. S., 76–78, 100–1, 156–57,
    160–71
Townsend, C., 106
Troll, L., 7

Vladek, B., 106
Veroff, J., 145
Vincente, L., 97
Vowler, R. M., 75

Wilson, S., 171
Worley, R. C., 49

Subject Index

Advocacy, by Church and Synagogue, 30
Age-in-place, 64
Ageism, by medical profession, 65
Aging, 3–14, 64, 79–81, 122–3
    changes during, 3–4, 122–3
    in the community, 8–9
    experience of, 3–4
    in the family, 6–8
    fears of dying, 4, 79
    maintaining identity, 4, 80–1
    midlife crisis, 4
    in modern society, 3–14
    in place, 8–9, 64, 81
    shift towards interiority, 3–4

Caretakers, 6–8, 44, 78, 82–3, 103–5, 130–34
    concerns, 78, 82–3, 103–5, 130–4
    daughters 6–7, 8
    families, 6–8, 44, 82–3, 103–5, 130–4
    wives, 7–8, 78, 82–3
Church and Synagogue, 27–37, 39–59, 75, 83–91, 108–18, 136–9, 143–57
    and the dying, 136–9
    as helping network, 29
    and the homebound, 33–4, 75, 83–91
    importance in programming, 27–9
    interfaith cooperation, 36–7, 39–59, 143–57
    and nursing home residents, 108–18
    role in serving elderly, 32–6, 64, 68–9, 110–8, 136–9
    (see also faith)
Church and Synagogue programs, 15–6, 29–37, 39, 45, 47–8, 66–7, 70–4, 84–94, 109–19, 136–9, 145–6
    duplication of services, 36–7, 85–6, 145–6
    for the dying, 136–9
    for homebound, 84–94
    influence of values, 15–6, 30, 45
    informal and formal, 31–2
    involvement of elderly, 32, 34, 66–7, 85–6
    for nursing home residents, 109–119
    types of, 29–37, 39, 47–8, 70–1, 84–6
    for well-elderly, 70–1, 73–4
    (see also ministries, holistic ministries)

Community, 8–9, 63–7, 80–4, 107
   change 8–9, 64–5
   and the homebound, 80–1,
     83–4
   and nursing home residents,
     107
   services for the dying, 134–6
   and well-elderly, 63–5
Community Advocacy Model,
   159–74
   community characteristics,
     161–5
   effects, 166–71
   general findings, 165–6
   introduction, 160–1
   summary, 171–4
Community Church, 39–59
   evaluation, 48–53
   program development, 41–8
   questionaire, 53–8
Continuity, 24, 27, 34, 81, 83–4
   for the homebound, 81, 83–4
   role of congregations, 24, 27, 34
Cooperation, 22, 36–7, 39–59, 77,
   85–6, 134–6, 143–157
   barriers to, 145–154
   Community Church, 39–59
   for dying, 134–6
   for homebound, 77, 85–6
   for individuals, 150–4
   levels of interaction, 148–50
   model for increased. See Com-
     munity advocacy model
   need for, 22, 143–5
   as organizations, 154–7
   See also interfaith efforts
Counseling, 22, 34, 66, 74, 83, 85–6
   by peers, 34, 66, 74, 85–6
   preference for clergy, 22, 83,
     136–8

Daughters, role in caring, 6–7, 8
Death, 4, 20–21, 121–2, 124–34
   preparing for, 20–21
Duplication of services, 36–7, 85–6,
   145–6

Dying, 4, 121–140
   community services, 134–6
   and families, 130–1, 133–4
   fear of, 4, 124
   identifying, 122–3
   needs of, 123–4, 132–3
   as process, 126–30
   program ideas, 139–40
   role of churches and syna-
     gogues, 136–9
   settings, 134–6

Elderly, 1–174
   characteristics, 5, 10, 12–3, 76–7
   and community, 8–9, 64–7,
     80–4
   and death, 4, 20–1, 121–2,
     124–34
   and dying, 121–40
   and families, 6–8, 44, 78,
     82–3, 103–5, 130–4, 138
   homebound, 75–96
   and holism, 15–25, 78
   involvement in programs, 32,
     34, 85–6
   in program development,
     15, 23
   living independently, 10, 12–3,
     65–6
   ministries for, 21–5, 70, 87–8
   in nursing homes, 10, 12–3,
     97–120
   old-old, 5–6
   population, 5
   and religion, 27–9, 67–8, 81
   and spiritual well-being, 15–25
   well-elderly, 63–74

Faith, 4, 27–9, 67–8, 81, 127–30
   importance of, 4, 27–9
   in dying, 127–30
   in homebound, 81
   in well-elderly, 67–8
   (see also holism)
Families, 6–8, 44, 78, 82–3, 103–5,
   130–4, 138

changes in structure, 6–7
concerns, 82–3, 103–5, 130–4
guilt in, 83, 138
role in caring, 7, 44, 78, 82

Holism, 15–25, 92–3, 117–8
concerns for the elderly, 16–8
definition, 16–8
and homebound, 92–3
life span perspective, 20–1
and nursing home residents,
117–8
in program development,
18–20, 92–3, 117–8
views on, 17–8
and spiritual well-being, 18
Holistic ministry, 22, 36–7, 73,
92–3, 117–8, 139–40
Homebound, 75–96
caretakers, 78, 82–4
characteristics, 75–8
community support, 83–4
concerns, 80–4
current programs, 84–91
concerns with the families,
82–3
needs, 78–79, 94–5
involvement, 85–6
program ideas, 93, 96
shut-ins, 77–84
Hospice movement, 134–5
Human dignity, 4, 21, 80
in homebound, 80
in preparing for death, 21

Identity of elderly, 4, 24
Interfaith efforts, 36–7, 39–53
Intergenerational relations, 72–3
Involvement of elderly, 32, 34,
66–7, 74, 83, 85–6
in peer counseling, 34, 66, 74,
83, 85–6
Independence, maintaining, 65–8

Life review, 24
Life span perspective, 20–1

Loss, 21, 66, 100–1, 124, 130–1,
133–4
coping with, 66, 131, 133–4,
138
types of, 100–1, 124
preparation for, 21, 124

Mainstreaming, 69, 72–3
barriers to, 69, 72
Ministries, 15–16, 21–5, 69–74,
87–8
holistic (see holistic ministry)
for homebound, 87–8
motives, 15–6
and spiritual well-being, 21–5
types of, 70, 87–8
for nursing home residents,
110–4
for well-elderly, 69–74

National Interfaith Coalition on
Aging, 18–20, definition of spiritual well-being, 19–20
Needs, 9–14, 65–8, 78–9, 94–5,
99–102, 104, 116–7, 123–4, 132–3
of elderly, 9–14
of dying, 123–4, 132–3
of homebound, 78–9, 94–5
of nursing home residents,
99–102, 104, 116–7
of old-old, 6
transportation, 5–6, 10
well-elderly, 65–8
Needs, identifying, 42–5, 76–9,
104, 116–7, 128–30
of dying, 128–30
of homebound, 76–9
of nursing home residents,
104, 116–7
of well-elderly, 42–5
Nursing homes, 97–8, 105–6
abuses in, 105–6
Nursing home residents, 10, 12–3,
97–120
characteristics, 98–9
concerns, 102–8

current programming, 108–11
needs, 99–102
new directions in programming, 114–5, 117
program ideas, 119–20

Older American Act, 11, 33
Old-Old, 5–6, 10, 12–13, 28, 48
characteristics, 5–6, 10, 12–13
and religion, 28
underrepresentation on church
boards, 48

Peer-counseling, 66, 74, 85–6
Program development, 15–25,
27–7, 42–8, 66, 92–3, 108,
114–18, 136–9, 147–57
collaborative, 147–57
for dying, 136–9
and holism, 18–20, 92–3, 117–18
influence of religious values,
15–16, 30
involvement of elderly, 15, 23,
32, 48, 66
interfaith, 36–7, 42–8
for nursing home residents,
114–17
by religious organizations,
21–22, 27–37
and spiritual well-being, 21–5,
108, 117–18
Program ideas, 73–4, 93, 96,
119–20, 139–40
for dying, 139–40
for homebound, 93, 96
for nursing home residents,
119–20
for well-elderly, 73–4
Programs, 108–10
in nursing homes, 108–10

Religion. See faith
Religious organizations. See
Church and Synagogue
Religious practices, 4, 21, 27–9
and very old, 4, 21, 28
and well being, 28–9
See also faith

Reminiscing, role of, 21, 24
Retirement, 6, 64
crisis, 6
planning for, 64
Retirement communities, 8,
64–5
moving to, 8, 64
relocation problems, 64–5

Snow-birds, 64
Spiritual well-being, 15–16, 18–25
concept of, 18–20
and holism, 19
and program development,
21–5
and dying, 128

Transportation needs, 5–6, 10,
12–13, 72

Very old, 4, 28
Visitation (by ministries), 33–5,
69, 75, 78–9, 85–8, 111–14
to homebound, 33–4, 69, 75,
85–88
in hospitals, 69
to nursing home residents,
111–14
role of, 33–5
to shut-ins, 78–9

Well-elderly, 63–74
in the community, 63–5
mainstreaming, 69, 72–3
needs, 65–8
role of Church and Synagogue,
68–9
types of programs, 70–1,
73–4
White House Conference on
Aging, 19
Widows, support groups, 74
Wives, role in caring, 7–8, 78,
82–3

Young old. See well-elderly